Living with a
Boxer

Edited by Sharon Hannibal

BARRON'S

THE QUESTION OF GENDER
The "he" pronoun is used throughout this book in favor of the rather impersonal "it,"
but no gender bias is intended at all.

ACKNOWLEDGMENTS

The publisher would also like to thank the following for help with photography: Pat Heath (Seefeld), Gill Davies (Kenbru), Daphne North (Carinya), Mrs. D. Eleri Davies (Elanbar), Terry and Maureen Donovan (Craigdon), George and Cathy Markos (von Bachbett), Charles and Margie Burton (Espirit), Joyce Baker Brown (Baker Brown), Hattie Garry (Florida Boxer Rescue), Karla Spitzer, Christina Ghimenti (Paw Print), Tracy Hendrickson (Sunchase) and Paula Rossman (Cinema).

First edition for the United States and Canada published by
Barron's Educational Series, Inc., 2002

All inquiries should be addressed to:
Barron's Educational Series, Inc.
250 Wireless Boulevard
Hauppauge, New York 11788
http://www.barronseduc.com

Library of Congress Catalog Card No. 2001095154

ISBN-13: 978-0-7461-5430-0
ISBN-10: 0-7461-5430-3

Printed in Singapore

9 8 7 6 5 4 3 2

CONTENTS

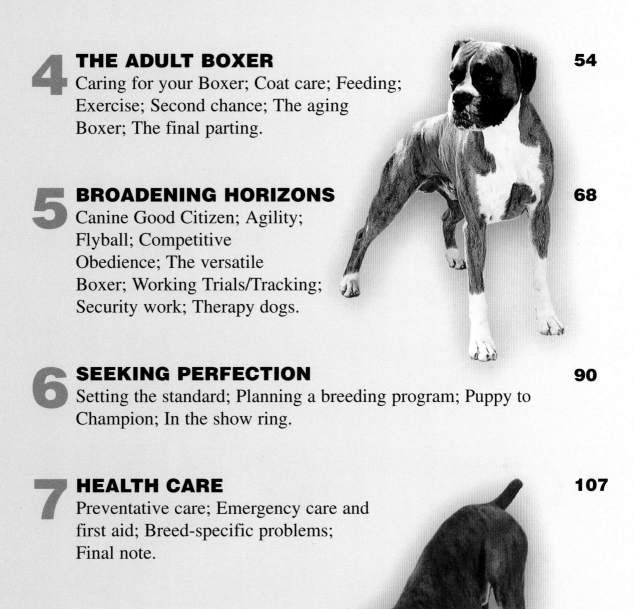

CHAPTER ONE

INTRODUCING THE BOXER

Noble, self-assured, fearless, the Boxer stands out as one of the most impressive of all breeds. But he has something else in his favor. The Boxer is lovable, friendly, and playful; in fact, he is a true clown at heart. These two sets of characteristics, which, at first glance, seem diametrically opposed to each other, sum up the true charm of the breed. The Boxer will be your loyal protector, but he will also be your family friend.

CREATING A SUPER-BREED

With many breeds, the exact origins are lost in the mists of time. Legend, informed guesswork, and speculation all play a part as fact and fiction mingle to create a colorful history. The Boxer has no pretensions to such a romantic past. Its history is recent, in relative terms, and well documented. For this is a breed that was made to measure, designed by a group of enthusiasts who decided exactly what their ideal dog should

look like, and what its temperament should be.

It all started in the Munich area of southern Germany in the closing years of the 19th century. A group of dog fanciers were keen to create a new super-breed, based on the broad-mouthed, big-hearted animals that had been used for bull-baiting. Although the sport was outlawed in the early 1800s, the brave, stocky dogs, known variously as Bullenbeisser (bull-biter) or Barenbeisser (bear-biter), according to their subgroup, were popular throughout northern Europe.

In 1887, one of the enthusiasts, George Alt, went to France and brought back a brindle and white bitch of the Bullenbeisser type. Flora, as she was known, was mated to a local dog of similar type. One of the resulting puppies, a white dog, was bought by one of George's friends, a Herr Lechner. The dog was named Lechner's Boxel.

In order to fix the type of dog they were producing, Lechner's Boxel was mated back to his mother. The litter was born in November 1893, and George Alt kept a white bitch puppy with brindle patches. She was known as Alt's Schecken. George was obviously concerned that breeding the line too closely could result in weakness, so he looked for a completely unrelated dog to sire the next litter. By luck, a Dr. Toenissen joined the group of Munich dog fanciers. He owned an English Bulldog called Tom, and this white dog with fawn patches, who looked more like a present-day Staffordshire Bull Terrier, was mated to Alt's Schecken.

THE FIRST BOXER

The birthday of the first Boxer is February 26th 1895 – the true starting point of a breed that has become a worldwide favorite. The litter sired by Tom, the Bulldog, produced a dark brindle dog called Flocki. He had white front legs, a white blaze, and a white muzzle.

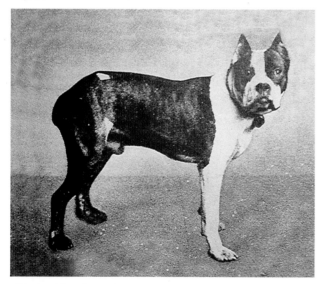

Flocki: The first Boxer to be registered.

This flashy looking dog caught the judge's eye at the first class scheduled for Boxers, which was at a show staged by the St. Bernard Club. Four Boxers were entered, and Flocki won, becoming the first Boxer entered in the German Stud Book.

The following year, the German Boxer Club was formed, and there was a total of 20 entries at their first show. Some of the dogs were white, some were black, and others were white with patches of brindle and fawn.

Although Flocki has earned his place in breed history, it was a bitch called Meta von der Passage who had the most long-term influence as an outstanding producer of top class Boxers. Her mother was Ch. Blanka von Angertor (sister to Flocki), and her father was Piccolo von Angertor (a grandson of Lechner's Boxel). In photographs, Meta does not look that stunning; she was long in the back, and she bears little resemblance to modern Boxers. But through her sons, in particular three top-class stud dogs by different sires, her bloodlines were spread worldwide.

BREED PIONEERS

Friederun and Philip Stockmann, a newly married couple living in Germany, shared a great passion for the new Boxer breed. They had saved up 1,000 marks to buy a house, but when, in 1911, a Boxer called Rolf von Vogelsberg, who was related to Meta von der Passage on both his mother's and his father's sides, came up for sale, they bought him instead.

During the First World War, the courageous Boxer was used as a trusted guard and messenger.

It certainly proved a wise investment. Rolf was shown throughout Europe and became a Champion. He became the foundation of the Stockmanns' famous von Dom kennel, and his offspring were exported to the U.S. where they became influential in the development of the breed.

In 1914, Philip Stockmann was called up to serve in the First World War. He left for the front taking Rolf and nine other Boxers with him. They joined a brigade which already had 50 Boxers attached to communication patrols. The dogs, working with handlers, were used to guard prisoners of war, making sure they were not armed and did not receive information from civilians. They were also trained to carry telephone cables through the trenches between command posts. The cable would be fastened to the dog's collar, and he would be "sent away" to where another handler would be waiting. The work was dangerous, as snipers would be on the lookout, so it was carried out in twilight. For obvious reasons, dark dogs, without conspicuous white markings, were preferred.

The service record of Boxers during the war was so distinguished that, in 1924, the breed was approved as a working police dog. But first, the breed club passed a new Breed Standard in which all-white dogs, or dogs with extensive white markings, were outlawed. This was because the white coloring was unacceptable in a guard dog.

THE BREED SPREADS

Rolf returned from his war duties unscathed. He went on to win more awards in the show ring, and to sire more outstanding stock before his death in 1920. His great-great-great-grandson, Ch. Sigurd von Dom, took over as Germany's top stud dog, and he was also a great showman. Frau Stockmann describes him in her book *My Life with Boxers:*

"He had a perfect body; front and hindquarters were correct, and his noble head was set on a strong, elegant neck. He represented the ideal Boxer, combining strength with speed and nobility. Sigurd was a first-class dominant sire, and each of his youngsters carried his quality and type. He had more than his share of vanity, loving to be photographed, and would sit still until the camera shutter clicked, then, with one jump, he would be gone."

When the Boxer was approved as a police dog, white dogs were ruled out as their coloring made them unsuitable for guarding work.

This was the dog that took America by storm. He was exported when he was five years old and enjoyed the most glittering show career in his new home, winning two Best in Show awards, 43 Working Groups and 54 Best of Breeds. He was the leading Boxer sire in the U.S. in 1936, and runner-up in 1939 and 1940. He was the first of America's Big Four, a quartet of hugely important dogs in the development of the breed in the U.S. The other three – Dorian von Marienhof (sire of 40 Champions), Lustig von Dom (sire of 41 Champions), and Utz von Dom (sire of 37 Champions) – were all grandsons of Sigurd.

In the U.K., the first British Boxer is recorded in 1911. Jondy was a granddaughter of Meta von der Passage, but she was never bred from. Interest in the breed was only sporadic until Charles Cruft scheduled the first class for Boxers in 1936. One of the great early enthusiasts was Mrs. Cecil Sprigge; she was instrumental in importing dogs from Europe, and she was made secretary of the British Boxer Dog Club, which was formed in 1936. Among the early imports was Burga von Twiel, who was in whelp to the illustrious Ch. Lustig von Dom. The stage was set for the breed to take off in the U.K. – but disaster struck with the outbreak of the Second World War.

THE WAR YEARS

Food rationing was only one of many hardships

Some Boxers were used for war work, but many more were destroyed.

endured during the Second World War, but it had a major impact on the dog-showing world. Breeders could no longer afford to keep large kennels of dogs and the number of registrations in all breeds dwindled. In the case of the Boxer, which was just emerging as a new breed in the U.K., registrations ground to a virtual standstill when only nine dogs were registered in 1942.

For some dogs, the war meant a new career, and, building on the success of the German War Dog Brigade in the First World War, a number of Boxers were used for war work.

Their duties mostly involved guarding, but there was also the famous American Boxer called Max, who joined a Paratrooper Unit when the U.S. became involved in the war. This fearless dog jumped from planes with the parachutists, and he earned his Wings after completing five successful jumps.

In Germany, the suffering was appalling. Some dogs were used by the armed forces, but many more were destroyed. In 1945, Philip Stockmann died in a prison hospital. His wife battled to keep their kennel going, but at the end of the war she was left with one granddaughter of the original von Dom Boxers to continue the line.

RECOVERY AND REVIVAL

Fortunately, dog-showing underwent a major revival in Britain in the post-war years. From the lowest point of registrations in 1942, the Boxer breed was swift to recover. By 1950, the number was 3,647, increasing to 5,592 in 1953.

Significantly, in 1946, the American Boxer breeder Jack Wagner was invited to judge the U.K.'s first Championship Show. In an article he wrote after the show, he gave a timely warning.

"We have been fortunate enough in the U.S.A. to have such famous imports as Int. Ch. Dorian von Marienhof, Utz von Dom, Lustig von Dom and Int. Ch. Sigurd von Dom to use as patterns and try to improve upon, and we are fortunate enough to have the latest Sieger, Int. Ch. Karlo v.d. Wolfsschlucht.

"I feel that the English breeders have to some degree lost sight of the fact that the Boxer is fundamentally a working dog and such a dog must be able to jump a 6- to 8-foot fence and must be able to travel at top speed for long distances. Such a dog cannot be found in the

Mastiff or the Bulldog. He must be in the order of a powerful terrier in the body build, with good length of leg, and a short, powerful back. In addition, as a companion and show dog, he should have the length of neck, head chiselling and reasonably narrow skull that makes for great beauty in a dog."

The British breeders took note, and, with the help of judicious imports from Europe and from the U.S., the breed prospered.

TOPS AND TAILS

The Boxer, loved and admired throughout the world, is one of the most distinctive looking of breeds. However, there are a couple of significant factors that affect the breed's appearance.

The natural-looking Boxer, with a full tail and uncropped ears.

The group of German enthusiasts who "designed" the Boxer, created a dog with cropped ears and a docked tail. The ears, set at the highest points of the sides of the skull, were to be cut rather long and tapering, and to be raised when alert. In Britain, ear-cropping was banned, and so, right from the start, the British Boxer looked very different. The ears were of moderate size, lying flat and close to the chin in repose, and falling forward with a definite crease when alert. Today, ear-cropping is still allowed in the U.S., in Germany, and in some of the other European countries, and so the two types remain.

The original Boxer's tail was docked short, and this was adopted by all the countries developing the new breed. Currently, docking is becoming increasingly controversial, and in many parts of Scandinavia it is banned. Obviously, this has a major impact on the general outline and appearance of the breed. In Britain and the U.S., the breed is still exhibited in the show ring with a docked tail.

THE WHITE BOXER

As we have seen, many of the original Boxers were white, or had extensive white markings, but these were outlawed when the Boxer was adopted as a police dog. Fawn or brindle Boxers were the two permitted colors, with white markings to enhance the appearance.

Today, all-white and near-white Boxers still appear in litters, but they cannot be shown in the ring, and they cannot be bred from. They are perfectly acceptable as companion dogs, although they do not resemble the typical, smart Boxer that most people imagine. A white Boxer will be sold at a greatly reduced price, but many breeders are reluctant to rear them. In common with all white animals, white Boxers have a predisposition to deafness, so white puppies may be euthanized at birth.

THE BOXER TODAY

The Boxer is now one of the most popular breeds in the world. In the U.S., registrations stand at nearly 39,000 a year, ranking as the ninth most popular breed. In the U.K., the Boxer is also the ninth most popular breed, with registrations of 10,573. The Boxer also enjoys great popularity throughout Europe.

In the show ring, the Boxer makes a stunning exhibit, but it is as a companion dog that the breed has really made its mark. The Boxer is an ideal family dog, loving all members of his human pack, while respecting and protecting his leader. He is easy to train, and, although the breed's working role as a security/guard dog has been phased out, the Boxer is successful in Competitive Obedience, Agility, and many of the other canine disciplines.

THE BOXER TEMPERAMENT

The breed's pioneers had a clear idea of what they wanted the Boxer to look like, but they also considered temperament to be of paramount importance. The American Breed Standard gives a very accurate description of the typical Boxer.

"Instinctively a 'hearing' guard dog, his bearing is alert, dignified and self-assured. In the show ring, his behavior should exhibit constrained animation. With family and friends, his temperament is fundamentally playful, yet patient and stoical with children. Deliberate and wary with strangers, he will exhibit curiosity, but most importantly, fearless courage if threatened. However, he responds promptly to friendly overtures honestly rendered. His intelligence, loyal affection and tractability to discipline make him a highly desirable companion."

As a glowing tribute to the Boxer, this cannot be improved. It is little wonder that those who have owned a Boxer never want to own any other breed.

The Boxer has a worldwide fan club.

CHAPTER TWO

PUPPY POWER

The Boxer has so much appeal that it is enormously tempting to rush out and buy a puppy. But that would be a big mistake. There are many important points to consider before taking on a dog of any breed – and if you are planning a commitment that will last a lifetime – between 12 and 14 years in the Boxer's case – it makes sense to do your homework before taking the plunge into ownership.

FINANCE

Firstly, and most obviously, do you have the money to buy a Boxer and to care for him properly? A purebred dog is an expensive item and you will need to cope with routine bills for feeding and health care. In addition, you may need to board your dog in kennels if you have to be away from home, and you may face big veterinary bills if your dog becomes ill or has an accident.

TIME

Do you have the time to devote to a dog? You may love the idea of owning a beautiful Boxer, but will your work schedule allow you to keep a relatively big dog that requires regular exercise? The Boxer is a breed that thrives on human companionship, and, if he is left alone for too long, not only will he become unhappy, he may well become deviant in his behavior. If you have to routinely leave your dog for longer than a three-hour stretch without any company, it is best to delay dog ownership until your timetable changes.

You must also find the time for your dog when you are at home. A Boxer needs at least two thirty-minute walks a day – rain or shine. Remember that the Boxer is an intelligent breed from working stock. He needs mental stimulation as well as physical exercise in order to be a contented, well-balanced companion.

Boxers are wonderful with children, but you must teach both puppy and child a sense of mutual respect.

LIFESTYLE

The Boxer is reasonably adaptable, but he does need an active owner to train him and exercise him. For those getting on in years, who prefer dog ownership at a slower pace, a smaller, less demanding breed may be more suitable.

The Boxer's short coat is easy to care for, and shedding does not cause a major problem. However, the house-proud should bear in mind that Boxers are "slobber dogs." The combination of having a short foreface and a well-padded muzzle means that saliva tends to accumulate – and a good shake will send it flying in all directions!

HAPPY FAMILIES

Boxers are wonderful family companions, and seem to really enjoy the company of children. Remember that a Boxer puppy grows into a very lively, powerful dog, and, for this reason, the breed is probably better suited to living with children that have passed the toddler age. Whatever age your family is, it is essential that both children and dog learn a mutual sense of respect (see page 34). Do not take on a Boxer puppy if you do not think you have the time to supervise him properly when he is with the younger members of the family.

LIVING WITH OTHER ANIMALS

If a puppy is brought up with other animals, there is rarely a problem. A Boxer puppy may be a little enthusiastic in his interactions to begin with, but the older animal will quickly put him in his place. If you already have a dog, you will need to exercise some tact and diplomacy in the initial stages to ensure relations get off to a good start (see pages 27-28).

MAKING THE DECISION

If you feel ready for Boxer ownership, you must now move from the general to the particular, and decide the age and type of Boxer that you want.

Companion or Show Prospect?

Doubtless you want a typical-looking Boxer, but, if you plan to show your dog, you will need to be far more demanding in your requirements (see Chapter Six). It is far better to plan for this in advance rather than trying to exhibit a Boxer of inferior quality and then becoming disillusioned with the whole show scene. You will almost certainly face a longer wait if you are looking for a show puppy.

Male or Female?

This is largely a matter of personal preference, although those planning a breeding program will obviously favor a bitch. For those looking for a companion, it is important to bear in mind that the male Boxer is a bigger, more powerful animal than the female. Measured from the shoulder, a male will be between 22.5 and 25 inches (57-63 cm), and the female will be between 21 and 23.5 inches (53-59 cm). Boxer males weigh 66-70 pounds (30-32 kg), and females are between 55 and 60 pounds (25-27 kg).

In temperament, there is little to choose between the sexes. Males can be a little more dominant, particularly during adolescence (see Chapter Three), and they can be rather boisterous at this stage. However, both male and female are equally loyal and affectionate.

The male Boxer is a big, powerful dog, and requires experienced handling.

If you opt for a female, you will have to cope with her seasonal cycle, which occurs every six to nine months. To be safe, you will need to keep her away from males during a period of around three weeks. There are specially-made sprays that can be used to disguise the bitch's scent at this time, but even with these, you must exercise extreme vigilance to prevent the birth of unwanted puppies.

If you do not plan to breed from your Boxer, it would be wise to consider neutering (see pages 52-53).

Color

There are two Boxer colors to choose from: fawn and brindle. But there is considerable variation of shades within these colors. A fawn

BOXER COLORS

Fawn with white markings.

Brindle with white markings.

Fawn with a black mask. This may not be as flashy as Boxers with white markings on their faces, but it is very distinctive.

White puppies do appear frequently in Boxer litters.

WHITE BOXERS: VICTIMS OF FASHION

Sheila Dawson was a successful breeder and exhibitor of Boxers and was working hard at establishing her own red line. She was asked if she could help to find a home for a white Boxer, and what she discovered changed her whole life. She gave up her own breeding program, and founded the White Boxer Rescue Center. This is now established as a national organization in the U.K., dedicated to the welfare of this much-misunderstood section of the breed.

"When I first came into the breed, I was told all the old wives tales and scare stories about white Boxers," said Sheila. "I was told that they were likely to be deaf, they were often blind, they had treacherous temperaments, and dreadful skin allergies. Apparently, the endless vet bills made them impossible to home, so it was far kinder to cull them at birth.

"When I agreed to help that first white Boxer, I was expecting to have these suspicions confirmed, but, instead, my opinion was changed for good. Harry was a picture of health, combining a wonderful nature with bounce and vigor – everything a Boxer should be. We had no problem finding a home for him, and equally surprising was the fact that thereafter, I started to be contacted by people looking for a white Boxer. This was the start of the White Boxer Rescue Center.

In 1992, we conducted a survey, sending out questionnaires to hundreds of Boxer owners in the U.K. We asked detailed questions about health, disabilities, and temperaments. The results provided the first direct comparison between white Boxers and colored Boxers, and we found that the only distinction was deafness. There was a 10 percent incidence of deafness in white Boxers compared with only 4 percent in colored Boxers. While there were sickly examples of all colors, there was absolutely no evidence to suggest that poor health, unsound temperament, or skin problems were more apparent in white Boxers.

"The facts about deafness are less worrying than the fiction. Overall, the occurrence of deafness is rare. It is virtually unheard of for there to be more than one deaf puppy in a litter. Markings, or lack of them, have little bearing on the problem, which is more common in some lines.

"It is important to understand that 80 percent of communication transferred to any dog is via body language and facial expression. That means a deaf dog loses out on only 20 percent of possible communication. As a result, deaf dogs are capable of living normal lives, and are able to do everything a hearing dog can. The White Boxer Rescue Center has successfully homed numerous deaf dogs, and provided training advice for many more.

"The thing that most people find surprising is that the breed was intended to be white. There were many white Champions, and, as long as the current fashion in the show ring is for flashy dogs (colored dogs with white markings), there will continue to be between one and three white pups born in most litters. If these puppies are not automatically culled at birth, they are raised with indifference – often without Kennel Club registration. Any puppy, regardless of breed or color, that is sold with so little concern or interest in its welfare, is more likely to end up in unsuitable circumstances."

Sheila emphasizes that her aim is not to achieve recognition in the show ring for white Boxers, but to educate exhibitors and breeders so that they stop passing white dogs on to the public as third-class Boxers, and appreciate that the white Boxer is simply a dog that is a different color.

There are a number of people who specifically want a white Boxer – and they certainly make first-rate family companions.

Boxer may be anything from a light tan to a rich mahogany. The brindle Boxer has black stripes on a background, which may range from light fawn to very dark brown. White markings are a feature of the breed, but, if you are looking for a show puppy, they should not exceed one-third of the entire coat.

If there are white or heavily-marked white puppies in the litter, think carefully before taking one on (see page 19). Although this is not the correct Boxer color, the dog's temperament will obviously be totally unaffected, and there are pet owners who are happy and proud to have a white Boxer.

An Older Dog

It may be that your circumstances are better suited to taking on an older dog. Sometimes, a breeder may come across a dog that turns out not to be of show quality. This type of dog may be sold to a pet owner on condition that it is not shown. Breeders have their reputation to guard, and would not want inferior stock being exhibited.

There are also adult dogs who come into Boxer Rescue and need rehoming. These dogs may take a little time to adjust to a new home, but the experience can be very rewarding (see pages 64-65).

FINDING A BREEDER

Regardless of whether you want a show dog or a companion, you must go to a breeder that is known for producing typical, healthy Boxers with sound temperaments. Boxer puppies are advertised in local newspapers as well as in the specialist canine press. However, the best route is to contact your national kennel club who will have details of a breed club in your area. The breed club secretary often has a register of puppies that are available, and you know that the breeders involved will be totally genuine. If you are planning to show your Boxer, it is a good idea to do a little more homework so that you have some understanding of what makes a show quality dog (see Chapter Six).

VISITING THE LITTER

There is no dog lover who can resist a litter of puppies, and you could be forgiven for wanting to take the whole lot home. However, it is important not to let your heart rule your head.

You are choosing a dog that will hopefully be with you for the next 12 years or more, so slow down, take a deep breath, and ask the breeder lots of questions. This is an ideal opportunity to learn about Boxers, as well as finding out how to look after a puppy.

There are certain observations that you should make before deciding to buy.

- The puppies should be housed in a light, airy environment which smells fresh.
- Droppings should be cleaned up, and there should be no evidence of leftover food.
- The bedding should be clean and comfortable.
- The puppies should be bold and friendly, ready to come forward and meet visitors.
- Each puppy should be well covered – neither too fat nor too thin.
- The coat should be clean, with no signs of dullness or dandruff. Dirt around the rear may indicate diarrhea.
- The eyes should be bright. There should be no discharge around the eyes or the nose.

- The inside of the ears should be clean and pink, with no evidence of foul odor.
- If the puppies' tails have been docked (this is usually done at around three days), the tips should be clean and well healed.
- You should have the opportunity to see the puppies with their mother.
- The sire and the dam should be heart-tested to ensure that they free from aortic stenosis (see page 127).

The breeder will also give you a thorough grilling to make sure that you will be a suitable owner. They will ask you about your family, your work schedule, and the plans you have for your Boxer puppy.

ASSESSING THE PUPPIES

In most cases, the breeder will allow you to visit the puppies when they are between four and six weeks of age. They generally go to their new homes at around eight weeks. The breeder may have already earmarked some puppies as having

The puppies should be lively and inquisitive.

show potential, but you should still be able to see the whole litter together.

Watch the puppies playing together and you will see their individual personalities begin to emerge. Generally, the puppies should be lively and inquisitive, and they should be happy to be handled. The breeder will obviously have spent a lot of time with the litter and will be able to tell you more about the individual puppies. Some breeders carry out temperament tests so that they have a more accurate picture of what each puppy is like. These generally take the form of a series of simple exercises to test reactions to noise, unfamiliar objects, handling, restraint, and response to basic training exercises, such as Sit, Down and Come. These tests cannot be carried out until the pups are around eight weeks of age.

In the meantime, you can tell a lot by meeting the puppies' mother. Although she may not look her best, as she is in the midst of rearing a litter, you will be able to see what her temperament is like. She should be friendly with visitors, and happy to show off her puppies. It is unlikely that you will meet the puppies' father as he probably lives some distance away, but you may be able to meet other close relatives. This will give some indication of how the puppies will turn out in terms of appearance and temperament.

If you are looking for a puppy with show potential, you will need to pay very close attention to conformation and movement (see Chapter Six). The pet owner who wants a nice, typical looking Boxer should look for a firm,

Watch the puppies playing together, and you will see their individual personalities begin to emerge.

strong back, a proud neck, and powerful, effortless movement. If the head appears rather pointed, this is a good sign. A pronounced occiput, which is the central point of the skull, is indicative of a well-balanced head when the dog is mature.

DOUBLE TROUBLE

You may be so entranced by Boxer puppies that you think it would be great to take on two puppies as company for each other. Resist the temptation, for it will only lead to trouble. There is a great deal of work involved in rearing and training a Boxer puppy, and you really must give him undivided attention. It is almost impossible to find the time to train two youngsters, and you will probably end up with two dogs that you cannot control.

Resist the temptation of buying two puppies at the same time.

If you want to have two Boxers, wait until your first dog is fully mature – around 18 months to two years – before getting a new puppy. The best match is generally a male and a female. Obviously, one will have to be neutered, but a pair of Boxers seem to live in harmony. Two males are rarely a good mix as they tend to vie with reach other for dominance.

PREPARING FOR YOUR PUPPY

Before your puppy arrives home, there are some important preparations to make to ensure your home and yard are safe and secure.

The best plan is to "think puppy." Get down to floor level and see what seems a likely target for a curious Boxer. Trailing electrical wires constitute a real hazard. A puppy will chew them, play tug-of-war with them, and run straight through them – so make sure they are firmly secured. Keep all household cleaners and bleaches well out of reach, and make sure your puppy cannot get at household plants. Beware of any fragile ornaments, fringes on upholstery and floor-length curtains. You must also attempt to teach your family to be tidy. A pair of shoes that are not put away may well prove irresistible.

Decide where your Boxer is going to sleep. Most people find the kitchen or the utility room to be the most convenient. Wherever you choose, the dog's bed or crate (see page 24) must be located in a warm room that is free from drafts.

The yard must be securely fenced. Boxers are not great escape artists, but, to begin with, your puppy will have no idea of boundaries and will squeeze through the smallest gaps as he explores his new environment. It is a good idea to allocate an area in the yard to use for toilet training (see Housebreaking, page 28).

CHOOSING EQUIPMENT

Dogs do not need a lot of equipment, but there are a few basic items you should purchase in advance.

Bed and Bedding

There is a huge variety of dog beds to choose from, ranging from wicker baskets and beanbags to padded and novelty dog igloos. However, your best bet is to start with a cardboard box and line it with some comfortable bedding. Your puppy is more than likely to chew his first bed – and he will certainly grow out of it – so it makes sense to keep cost to a minimum.

As your Boxer gets bigger, a plastic, kidney-shaped bed is a good buy. These are practically indestructible and they are easy to clean. They come in lots of different sizes, so you will be able to find one that fits your Boxer when he is fully grown.

You can use old towels or blankets for bedding. But it is probably more convenient to buy some purpose-made synthetic fleece bedding. Dogs love it, and it has the advantage of being machine washable and quick-drying.

Crate

An indoor crate is becoming an increasingly popular type of accommodation; it can make rearing a puppy a great deal easier if it is used correctly (see Crate-Training, page 29). If you decide to invest in a crate, make sure you buy one that is big enough to accommodate an adult Boxer in comfort. The minimum size would be 31 inches long (77.5 cm), 27 inches (67.5 cm) high, and 26 inches (65 cm) wide.

Collar and Lead

Start off with a lightweight, adjustable collar. This minimizes the feeling of restraint around the neck, and you can alter the size as your puppy grows. It also helps if the lead is not too

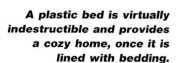

A plastic bed is virtually indestructible and provides a cozy home, once it is lined with bedding.

big and heavy, but you must make sure it has a secure trigger fastening.

When your Boxer is fully grown, you can choose from the vast array of collars and leads that are available. Beware of nylon leads, which can chafe your hand if your dog pulls. Chain leads may look smart, but they are very uncomfortable and inflexible for the handler.

ID

All dogs should wear an identity tag, giving contact details. Start off with a lightweight tag for your puppy's first collar, and, when he is wearing a more substantial collar, you can get a heavier, engraved disk.

You may decide to have your puppy microchipped. This is a small implant, containing a unique number, that can be scanned to give contact details if your dog ever gets lost. The vet will carry out this simple task.

Grooming Equipment

It is important that your Boxer gets used to being groomed from an early age. A soft bristle brush will be sufficient to begin with. Your Boxer's nails will need trimming on a routine basis, so you will need some nail clippers. A toothbrush and canine toothpaste will complete your grooming kit.

Toys

There are plenty of dog toys to choose from, and your Boxer puppy will love them all. Before buying a toy, make sure it is 100 percent safe. If a puppy can get the squeaker out of a toy or is

Make sure the toys you buy are safe and tough.

able to chew it into pieces, it could be very hazardous. The best puppy toys are the cotton rope tugs, and toys that are made of hard rubber.

CHOOSING A VET

Obviously, you hope you have chosen a fine, healthy puppy, but this does not mean that you should delay finding a vet until you need one. At all events, it is a good idea to have your puppy checked over within the first couple of weeks. You will need to start his vaccinations, and you will need to continue his worming program.

The puppy's breeder may be able to recommend a vet in your area, or you may have dog-owning friends or neighbors who can suggest an office. Before making an appointment, go to the office and chat with the receptionist or one of the vets. Find out what facilities are available, how the appointment system is run, and what arrangements are made for emergency care. You may also want to find out if alternative therapies are offered.

The big day arrives when it is time to bring your puppy home.

THE NAME GAME

Finally, you will need to choose a name for your puppy. In most households, this debate goes on for weeks – and it is all part of the fun of taking on a new puppy. Obviously the final decision is a matter of personal preference, but there are a couple of points to bear in mind.

- Do not opt for a name that is long-winded or difficult to say. You might think that "Napoleon" sounds distinguished, but, by the time you get it out, your puppy could be miles away!
- Try to be consistent in the way you call your dog. "Sammy," "Sam," and "Sambo" may mean the same to you, but, to a puppy who is working purely on the sound of the word, it could be very confusing.

Make sure all discussions are finalized before your puppy arrives home. If you are still in the planning stages and start calling him "Puppy" as a temporary measure, he will think that is his name . . .

COLLECTING YOUR PUPPY

At last, the big day arrives when it is time to collect your puppy. If possible, make arrangements to go in the morning, and then you will have as much time as possible to settle your puppy in his new home before nightfall.

You will need to take an adult assistant with you to hold the puppy on the journey home. Take a soft towel for the puppy to nestle into, and some paper towels in case of accidents.

Before you leave, the breeder will give you a copy of your puppy's pedigree and his kennel club registration documents. You will probably be given a sample of the diet the litter has been eating, which will last you over the next couple of days.

With any luck, your puppy will be lulled to sleep as you drive home. If it is a hot day, make sure there is adequate ventilation in the car, and, if it is a long journey, break it up with regular stops. You can give your puppy some water to drink, and allow him to enjoy some fresh air, but, remember, you cannot put him down on the ground or allow him to meet other dogs until he has completed his vaccinations.

ARRIVING HOME

Your Boxer puppy will be glad to get out of the car – but there is a strange new world awaiting him, and even the most confident pup will feel frightened and insecure to begin with.

Start off by taking your puppy into the yard. Give him a chance to sniff and explore, and he will also have the opportunity to relieve himself. The family will be desperate to meet the new arrival, but give him a little while to find his feet before loading on more new experiences.

If you have children, allow them to meet the puppy and have a little game, but make sure no one gets overexcited. It is best if all interactions with puppies and children are at ground level, and then there is no risk of the puppy being dropped and injured.

Next, take your puppy into the house. Show him where his bed is, and allow him to take in his new environment. He will probably be

Give your puppy a chance to explore the yard.

hungry, so let him have some of the food the breeder has given you. Some Boxer puppies will wolf this down, others will feel too worried to settle down and eat. If your puppy does not want his meal, do not worry. Throw it away, and try again in a couple of hours. A puppy may not eat properly for the first 24 hours, but he will come to no harm, as long as fresh drinking water is available.

THE RESIDENT DOG

If you already have a dog, you will need to supervise introductions. Go out into the yard, as the adult dog will feel less territorial there than when he is the house. Allow the two dogs to meet each other. They will sniff and circle a round each other; the puppy is likely to be quite submissive in his behavior. Try not to interfere; it is best to allow the dogs to communicate in their own language.

If the adult dog gives a warning growl, do not become overprotective with the puppy. The adult needs to establish his status, and the pup needs to respect him. To begin with, supervise the two dogs when they are together. Some adults are very playful with puppies, others are less tolerant, but, in most cases, they will quickly work out their relationship with each other.

Puppies are such attention-seekers that it is all too easy to focus on the pup and ignore the adult. This is the time when trouble could arise if the older dog feels he is being usurped. Make sure you have some special times with your adult dog so that he feels he is just as important as ever. Play some games with him, run through some training exercises, and, as your puppy will be too young to go out for walks, you can make exercise sessions quality times for your adult dog.

FELINE RELATIONS

Boxers are good-natured dogs, and, with the right training, they will learn to live in harmony with all the family pets – including the cat. A Boxer puppy is generally bold and inquisitive, and he will be only too keen to go up and make friends. This exuberant approach will not be to the cat's liking, so it is important to intervene so that relations get off on the right footing.

- Hold your puppy in your lap, and call the cat over to you.
- Curiosity will get the better of her, and the cat will not be able to resist coming over to investigate.

Not all cats are this tolerant, but if you supervise initial interactions, both puppy and cat will learn to live peacefully together.

- Restrain your puppy so that he does not attempt any boisterous overtures and talk reassuringly to them both.
- Make sure there is a high vantage point for your cat to retreat to if she feels the need.

For the first few days, repeat these introductions, gradually reducing your hold on the puppy. As they get used to each other, the novelty will wear off, and you will find that they start to accept each other's presence. Some Boxers and cats become great friends, even sharing a bed, but, even if your pets do not reach these dizzy heights of harmony, they will certainly learn to live alongside each other in peace.

HOUSEBREAKING

This starts literally the moment your puppy arrives home and you let him out in the yard. Take your puppy to the area you have allocated for toilet-training, and, when he performs, give lots of praise.

An eight-week-old puppy will need to relieve himself at very regular intervals throughout the day. As a general guide, you should take him out

- as you get up in the morning
- after every meal
- after a play session
- every time he wakes from a sleep
- as you go to bed at night

A puppy will need to go out at least every two hours, so to begin with, you will need to keep a close eye on the clock. Your puppy will show signs that he needs to relieve himself by becoming restless, sniffing the floor, and circling. Be vigilant, and you will prevent accidents.

When you take your puppy out, go to the toilet area and give a command such as "Be clean." In time, the pup will learn to associate the command with the correct response. He will also learn that he goes to this part of the yard to relieve himself. You must stay with your puppy until he has performed, and then give him lots of praise. Boxers are quick learners, and, if you work hard at supervising your puppy, you will find that he is housebroken in no time. Make sure you keep the toilet area scrupulously clean, particularly if you have children.

You cannot expect an eight-week-old puppy to be clean during the night. So put some newspapers down on the floor near his bed so that your puppy has a place to go. As he matures, he will be able to wait until you let him out in the morning. If you use a crate (see page 24), you can speed up this process.

Many owners make the mistake of relaxing their efforts with housebreaking after a few weeks. Your puppy may have got the idea, but he still needs you to think for him. Keep taking him out at regular intervals, always praise him when he responds, and you will end up with a Boxer that is 100 percent clean and reliable.

CRATE-TRAINING

If you have decided to use a crate, get it ready before your Boxer arrives home. Line it with bedding, and put a toy in there so that it looks inviting. Let your puppy go and explore the crate, leaving the door open. Stroke him while

Take your puppy outside at regular intervals and he will soon learn to be clean in the house.

he is in the crate, giving him lots of reassurance. You can also try feeding your puppy in his crate so that he learns to associate his new "home" with a good experience.

Puppies get tired very easily, so, when your puppy is feeling sleepy, put him in his crate. Close the door, but stay with him. In most cases, a puppy will be glad of finding a safe, peaceful place to settle, and it will not be long before he looks at his crate as his own special den. The big advantage for the owner is that the puppy is safe and secure at times when he cannot be supervised. At nighttime, and when you have to go out, you know that your puppy cannot get into any mischief.

Never use the crate as a means of punishment, and do not let your puppy stay in the crate for long periods during the day. It is essential that your puppy sees the crate as his chosen place. In fact, many Boxers will voluntarily seek out their crate when the door is left open and settle down in there of their own free will.

A crate can also be used as an aid to housebreaking. When you have to leave your puppy for any length of time, take up the bedding from the front third of the crate and line it with newspaper. Dogs hate to foul their own beds, so your puppy will make sure that any mess he makes will be on the newspaper. As he gets older, he will try not to mess in his crate, but will wait until he is let out.

CHEWING

All puppies need to chew: it is their way of exploring a new object, it gives them something to do, and, during teething, it helps to relieve discomfort. If you provide suitable toys, it will not only help your puppy's development, it will cut down on the damage he will do if he gets hold of inappropriate objects. If you see your puppy with something that is forbidden, take it from him and immediately substitute it with one of his own toys.

THE FIRST NIGHT

This is the moment that all new puppy owners dread. One moment your puppy seems exhausted, but, when he is put in his bed and left alone, he develops a new lease of life, barking and whining for attention. Looking at it from the puppy's point of view, he has every reason to cry. For the first time, he has been left to sleep without the warmth and comfort of his littermates, and, to add insult to injury, his new-found family has suddenly deserted him.

You can take pity on your puppy and go

It is almost impossible to harden your heart when a puppy cries at night, but, if you give in to him, you could be storing up trouble for the future.

down to comfort him, or even take him into your bedroom. But, in many ways, you are only prolonging the agony. Your puppy needs to learn that it is OK to be left, or he will become so dependent on you that he never learns to cope on his own.

The best plan is to make sure your puppy is safe and comfortable when you leave him, and then ignore his cries. If you are using a crate, you can have complete peace of mind as you know your puppy cannot get into trouble. Some people find that leaving a radio on, with the volume turned low, helps the puppy to settle.

In most cases, it only takes a couple of nights for the puppy to understand the routine and to give in gracefully.

ESTABLISHING A ROUTINE

Dogs are creatures of habit and they thrive on routine. Your Boxer puppy will settle into his new home much more quickly if you establish a pattern for the day.

Mealtimes

When your puppy first arrives home, he will need four meals a day, so this can provide a format for your day. Feed the first meal as you get up, the second at midday, the third late afternoon, and the final meal at around 8 p.m.

It is important to feed the diet your puppy has been used to, at least to begin with. The combination of introducing new food and the stress of moving homes is almost certain to result in an upset stomach. Make sure that fresh water is available to your puppy at all times.

The number of meals should be gradually reduced as your puppy grows. By 12 weeks, three meals will be sufficient. The afternoon meal is the easiest one to miss out, and you can compensate by feeding the evening meal a little earlier. By six months of age, your Boxer should be fed twice a day.

There are many different types of dog food available, ranging from canned and complete diets to the more traditional meat and biscuits. The choice comes down to convenience and budget. While your puppy is growing, it is essential not to economize on your food bills. Your Boxer needs a top quality, balanced diet in order to mature into a fit, healthy adult.

Unless you have a good reason, you would be advised to stick to the diet recommended by

Do not introduce any changes in the diet while your puppy is settling in.

your puppy's breeder who will have vast experience in feeding Boxers. If this diet does not suit your puppy – he may keep getting diarrhea, or he may just show lack of interest in his food – consult your vet before making a change. If a new diet is recommended, do not make an immediate switch or you will just add to your puppy's problems. Introduce the new diet gradually, adding just a little of the new food at every meal without increasing the overall ration, until you have made a smooth transition.

EXERCISE

First-time owners often think that Boxer puppies need lots of exercise. This is far from the truth. It is all too easy to put too much strain on growing joints by overexercising, so never try to push your puppy too hard. For the first six months, a Boxer will get sufficient exercise just playing in the yard. Obviously, he needs to go out to be socialized (see page 40) once he has completed his vaccination course, but a ten-minute lead walking session will be ample. Try to limit the times he walks up and down stairs, and lift him in and out of the car.

When your Boxer is over six months, you can step up his exercise to include a ten-minute free run, as well as his lead walking. Wait until your Boxer is fully mature before changing this routine (see page 61).

GROOMING AND HANDLING

A Boxer puppy will need very little grooming, but he should get used to being handled and to the feel of the brush. Set aside a few minutes each day, and give your puppy a quick brush over. Hold him with one hand, and brush with smooth, firm strokes. Do not turn it into a battle of wills; just spend enough time so that your puppy gets used to the idea.

He must also accept being handled all over; no-go areas are not permitted.

• Stroke your puppy all over, moving down his stomach and around to his hindquarters.

• Lift up his paws, one by one, so that you can look at the pads.

• Stroke your puppy on the head, and then look into his ears.

• Open his mouth to look at his teeth.

When your puppy is happy with this routine, ask a friend to "go over" him in the same way

Accustom your puppy to the routine of being groomed.

so that he is used to being handled by strangers. This routine examination is of the utmost importance for two reasons.

• Your puppy accepts that you have the right to handle him. This will mean that he will tolerate a vet's examination, and, if he is to go into the show ring, he will accept being handled by the judge.

• A regular routine examination means that you will spot any signs of trouble at a very early stage.

Nails

The breeder will have trimmed your puppy's nails when he was very young and still suckling from his mother. Puppies' nails are very sharp and can cause considerable distress to the dam if she becomes scratched and sore.

You will need to keep a check on the nails to make sure they do not grow too long. If they need trimming, use guillotine nail clippers and just remove the nail tip. If you trim back too far, you will cut into the quick, which will bleed. You will probably need someone to hold the puppy while you clip the nails. If you do not feel confident, ask for the help of an experienced dog owner, or your vet will do the job for you.

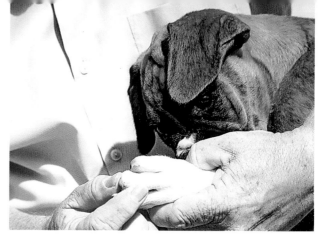
Lift up your puppy's paws and examine the pads and nails.

Teeth

Your puppy will lose his first "milk" teeth when he is around four months of age. At this time the gums often become sore and swollen, and your puppy will need to relieve the discomfort by chewing. Make sure you provide safe toys or dental chews for your puppy at this time. You may also notice that teething has a strange effect on your Boxer's ears. A slight sagging may be evident in ears that have been cropped. With natural, dropped ears, the carriage may become erratic, with one or both ears "flying" at a strange angle. This is only a temporary phase, and the ears will return to normal once the adult teeth have come through.

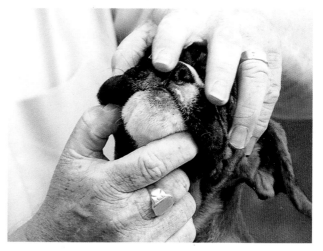
Stroke the pup's head and then check the ears.

Although your puppy's new adult teeth will be glistening white, it is a good idea to get him used to teeth-cleaning sessions. You can buy special meat-flavored dog toothpaste, so your Boxer will like the experience. Use a long-handled toothbrush or a nail-brush, and rub the teeth gently.

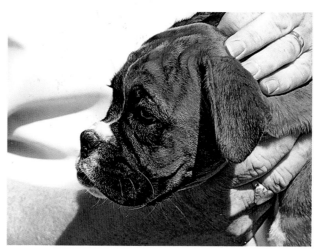
The puppy must get used to having his mouth opened, and his teeth checked.

Worming

The breeder will have started a worming program, and will have given you details of this when you collect your puppy. Make sure you make a note of when the next treatment is due. If you need further advice, contact your vet (see Chapter Seven).

BOXERS AND CHILDREN

Children and puppies make great playmates, but, for the relationship to work, both must learn a sense of respect for each other. Children must understand that a puppy is a living creature and cannot be pulled around like a soft toy. They must also learn that a puppy needs to

Teach your puppy to take a treat gently.

rest, and when he is sleeping he must never be disturbed.

Until now, your puppy has only played with his littermates, biting at them and rolling them over in a general rough-and-tumble. Your puppy has to learn to play gently with his human family. He must learn that he cannot use his teeth, and he cannot jump up. This may seem relatively unimportant when your pup is only eight weeks old, but, as he gets bigger and stronger, you will be glad you started his lessons early.

Play Gently

The first step is to teach your Boxer the "Gently" command.

- Hold a treat in your hand and offer it to the pup.
- If he takes it, say "Gently," praise him, and give him the treat.
- If he is at all rough, say "No," and start again.
- When your puppy has mastered the "Gently" command, allow a child to give a treat under supervision.

Taking Toys

It is easy for toys to become a source of trouble. A puppy can get confused as to which are his toys and which toys belong to the children. This is matter of teaching your children to put away their toys. If your pup gets hold of one of their toys, take it away and immediately give him one of his own toys.

It is fun for a child and a puppy to play with a toy together, but this is a game that can quickly get out of hand, with the puppy becoming overexcited or too possessive.

- Sit with the pup and give him a toy. Let him play with it for a few moments, and then take it back, using a command such as "Leave." Be firm, but do not pull it from your puppy's mouth or he will think you are playing tug-of-war.
- As soon as you have the toy, give your puppy a treat and praise him, and give him the toy back. In this way, your puppy learns he has nothing to lose by letting you have the toy – in fact, he has quite a lot to gain from it!
- When you are confident that your pup is responding to the "Leave" command, let a child try the exercise under supervision.

Food for Thought

Food can be a touchy area, but a dog who is possessive about his food bowl is a positive menace.

- While your puppy is eating, drop a couple of treats into his bowl. Instead of seeing your hand as a threat, he will welcome the intervention.
- Next, command "Leave" when your puppy is feeding and take the bowl away.
- Reward him instantly with a treat and return the bowl.
- When you are 100 percent sure that your puppy is responding correctly, allow a child under supervision to repeat the exercise.

Your puppy needs to learn that all members of his family can take his toys or his food. Obviously, the lesson must never be abused to tease the puppy, which is why adult supervision is essential.

FIRST LESSONS

Although you do not want to overtax your puppy, there is no reason why you should not start work on some basic training exercises. This will mean that you will have more control over your puppy by the time he has completed his vaccination course and is ready to venture into the outside world (see page 42).

The secret is to keep training sessions very short, as puppies have a limited concentration span, and to make them fun. If your puppy sees his lessons as quality time spent interacting with his owner, he will make rapid progress.

CLICKER TRAINING

This method of training, which is based on sound association, is becoming an increasingly popular way of working with animals. The clicker is a small plastic box, which, when pressed with the thumb, makes a "click."

This signals a correct response and the pup learns that a treat is coming. Eventually, the sound of the clicker becomes a reward in itself.

The advantage of the clicker is that you can reward your puppy the instant he responds correctly. It is a "yes" marker, telling the pup he is performing well.

Clicker training has been used with great success in many of the canine disciplines, including show training, Obedience and Agility. It is also a great way of teaching your pup fun tricks.

ESTABLISHING MUTUAL RESPECT

Sometimes a Boxer puppy can become possessive about his toys.

Supervise play sessions ensuring that the pup does not get too excited – and gives the toy up at the end of the game.

Sit

This is the simplest exercise to teach, and your Boxer will pick it up in no time.

- Get a treat at the ready and hold it in your hand, just above your puppy's head.
- As he looks up at the treat, he will naturally lower himself into a Sit.
- Click and reward your puppy with the treat.
- If your puppy is reluctant to go into the Sit, keep holding the treat above his head, and with your other hand, apply a little gentle pressure to his hindquarters.
- When you are getting an instant response, introduce the verbal command "Sit" as your puppy goes into position, then click and reward.

You can also practice this exercise at mealtimes, holding the food bowl just out of reach until your puppy sits. You will be amazed how quickly he learns!

Down

This is an extension of the Sit exercise, and, if your Boxer is keen on his treats, he will soon get the idea.

- Show your puppy a treat, and then lower it toward the floor.
- Your puppy will follow his nose, and his forequarters will go down as he tries to get at the treat.
- In order to balance, his hindquarters will follow, and your puppy will go into the Down position. Click and reward.
- Keep practicing and your puppy will start to go into position more quickly. Introduce the

Hold a treat above your puppy's head (above), and as he looks up he will naturally go into the Sit position (below).

Lower a treat toward the ground, and your pup will follow it, going into the Down position.

verbal command "Down" when he is responding instantly.

If your puppy is reluctant to go into the Down, there is another method you can try.

• Sit on the floor, and bend one leg to make a tunnel.

• Place your pup between your legs, and then lower the treat to the floor on the far side of the "tunnel."

• As your puppy tries to get at the treat, he will have to lower himself into the Down to get under your leg. Click and reward as soon as he is in the correct position.

Try this method for a few training sessions, introducing the verbal command. When your puppy has got the idea, you can revert to the first method – which is a lot less backbreaking!

Come

When your puppy first arrives home, he will follow you everywhere. Puppies instinctively follow their dam, and this allegiance will be transferred to the breeder, and then to you. It is a good idea to capitalize on this and start some basic recall training.

• Get some treats and your clicker, and call your puppy – "Ben, Come" – from a pace away.

• When he responds, click and give a treat, and then step back a couple of paces.

• Call your puppy to you, and when he reaches you, click and give a treat.

• Gradually increase the distance at which you leave your puppy before you give the recall command.

This exercise can be repeated at various times

Capitalize on your puppy's instinct to follow by working on his recall training.

throughout the day, and, in time, you can try calling your pup from one room to another.

Collar and Lead Training

The first task is to get your Boxer used to wearing a collar.

• Fit the collar, allowing two fingers to fit underneath when it is fastened.

• Have a game with your puppy so that you distract his attention from the collar.

• It is a good plan to feed him, as he will be so busy eating, he will forget to scratch and worry about the collar.

The first stage is to get your puppy used to wearing a collar and being on the lead.

- After ten minutes take the collar off, and repeat the same exercise two or three times a day. You will soon find that your Boxer accepts his collar without question.

Do not start lead training until you are confident that your puppy is happy with his collar.

- To start with, fasten the lead, and allow your puppy to walk around trailing the lead. Make sure it does not get caught up on any obstacles.
- Pick up the end of the lead, and follow your puppy wherever he chooses to go.

The next stage is to train your puppy to walk with you on the lead.

- Arm yourself with treats and with the clicker, and walk with your puppy on the lead, encouraging him to follow.
- Every time he gets into the correct position, walking beside you on a loose lead, click and then reward with a treat.
- As your Boxer gets used to clicker training, the treats can be given randomly as the "click" will serve as the reward.
- If your puppy tries to forge ahead, stop in your tracks, and call your puppy back to your side. Do not move off again until the puppy is in the correct position.
- If your puppy tries to drag behind, do not pull him to keep up with you. Stop and call your puppy to you, using a treat if necessary. When he is in the correct position, move off, using lots of verbal encouragement.

Stay

When you teach this exercise, keep it separate from Recall training, so the puppy does not get confused. The last thing you want is a hesitant response to the "Come" command, or a puppy who keeps breaking position when he is commanded to "Stay."

- Start off with your puppy on lead in the Sit.
- Take one pace away, and command "Stay." Back up your verbal command with a hand signal, palm held flat toward the puppy.
- Step back and praise your puppy quietly while he remains sitting.
- It is useful to introduce a release command, such as "OK," so your puppy knows the exercise is over. You can then reward him with a treat.

Build up the Stay exercise in easy stages.

• Repeat the exercise, stepping back a little
  further each time you leave your puppy. You
  can then progress to stepping to the side of
  him and behind him so that he becomes really
  secure when he is told to "Stay."

In time, you can progress to training this
exercise off-lead.

Car Travel

It is essential to have a dog that travels quietly
and calmly in the car. It helps if you have a

specific area in the car for your Boxer, such as in
the rear in a crate, or behind a dog guard. Many
puppies are lulled to sleep by the motion of the
car, but there are also the awkward customers
who make a fuss, barking or whining. The best
course of action is to ignore the protests. Put on
the radio or sing a song, and carry on as if
nothing was happening. For both your sakes,
make the journey short. When your puppy is
fully vaccinated, you can go to the park so that
a car trip is associated with an enjoyable
experience. Generally, Boxers soon learn to enjoy
car travel, and, as they like to be part of all the
family activities, they don't need to be asked
twice when an outing is offered.

When you get to your destination, make sure
your Boxer is trained to "Wait" when you open
the door. He must never leap out unless you
give the command. Unfortunately, this has been
the cause of too many accidents.

Sometimes puppies are a little carsick to begin
with. In most cases, they grow out of this,
particularly if you are careful not to feed your
pup before an outing. If the problem persists,
consult your vet, who will be able to prescribe
some medication.

SOCIALIZING YOUR BOXER

This is the most important part of your Boxer's
education, and you should devote as much time
as possible to it. A puppy is able to absorb and
learn from a variety of experiences, and this will
affect his whole outlook on life. A Boxer that
has gone out and about, meeting different
people, different animals, and encountering

A well-socialized puppy will grow up to be tolerant and adaptable.

a wide range of sights and sounds, will grow into a well-balanced adult. Given the correct supervision, he learns that there is nothing to fear, and so there is no need to become either aggressive or fearful.

Early Days

Early socialization can begin as soon as your puppy arrives home. Although the litter may have been reared in a home environment, there will still be lots of new experiences to get used to. We take household equipment – the vacuum cleaner, the washing machine, and the television – entirely for granted. But they can seem quite alarming to a puppy who is feeling lost and lonely without the support of his littermates.

If your puppy is alarmed by anything in the house, do not rush to pick him up and cuddle him. He will think there really is something to be frightened of. The best plan is to get some treats or a toy, and distract your puppy's attention from the machine. When he is feeling confident again, allow him to go up and sniff the machine. Give him lots of encouragement, and then reward him with another treat or a game.

With most puppies, particularly outgoing Boxer puppies, these sort of alarms are very fleeting, and with correct handling your puppy will forget he was ever frightened.

Puppy Parties

You cannot venture into the outside world until your puppy has completed his vaccination course. In the past, this meant that socializing with other dogs had to be delayed until 12 to 14 weeks of age. Now many veterinary practices organize puppy parties specifically for this age group where pups can meet each other in complete safety. This is a very valuable experience as the puppies can play together without being overshadowed by more intimidating adult dogs.

Training Club

When your puppy is fully vaccinated, you may consider enrolling at a training club. Do some research before signing up, as training classes can vary considerably. Ideally, you want to find a club which uses positive reinforcement for training. That means the dogs are rewarded with a treat or a game if they do the right thing. The aim is to work with a dog who wants to cooperate rather than being forced into good behavior. Hopefully, the club will also help you with clicker training.

A training club gives the opportunity for your dog to mix with other dogs, and to work in an environment that is full of distractions. You will get the benefit of the instructor's advice, and you can also enjoy a get-together with other "doggy" people.

The Outside World

There are numerous opportunities to socialize your Boxer – and you should take advantage of them all. Even if you are only going down the street to buy a newspaper, take your puppy. The more he experiences, the more confident and

Take your puppy out as much as possible so that he can experience a variety of different situations.

settled he will become. Try to include some of the following ideas in your socialization program.

• Take your puppy to a relatively quiet shopping area and find a bench. Sit with your puppy at your side, and just let him watch the passing scene. Boxer puppies are irresistible, so you will almost certainly get people coming up to talk to you both. This will help your puppy get used to being approached by strangers.

• Go to a bank (they usually allow dogs) so that your puppy can get used to going in and out of doors, and then line up. This may sound unexciting, but you are showing him a new interior environment which looks and smells very different to home.

The well-socialized Boxer is a pleasure to own.

- Walk past a building site or a place where repairs are being carried out on the road so that your puppy hears and sees heavy machinery in use.
- Go to a railway station and get a ticket, so that you can take your puppy on to the platform. The crowds of people, the hurly-burly of carts full of luggage, and the noise of the trains is a formidable experience.
- When you go to the local park, find out where the play area is. Allow your puppy to sit and watch children playing.
- In the summer, there are always outdoor fundraising events which are full of activity. If you live in the country, go to a country fair and then your puppy will be able to meet a variety of livestock in pens, as well as mingling in the crowd with lots of different people.

Obviously, you do not want to intimidate your puppy by piling on too many new experiences. Start with small outings in quiet areas, and then you can become more adventurous as your puppy finds his feet. If your Boxer is concerned by anything he sees, never try to drag him past. Equally, it is important not to be too sympathetic. Encourage your puppy forward, using a treat, and let him have a second look at whatever he is worried about. In most cases, your Boxer will be happy to move on. If he has shown fear of something, do not go out of your way to avoid it on future occasions. It is important that your puppy learns there is nothing to be frightened of.

CHAPTER THREE

THE ADOLESCENT BOXER

Hopefully, you will enjoy all the stages of your Boxer's life from puppyhood through to old age. However, there is no doubt that some phases will present more of a challenge than others – and adolescence probably ranks as the most testing time.

With good care and management your Boxer has grown from a loveable, mischievous pup to a good-looking, outgoing youngster that has become an integral part of the family. Physically, your Boxer is nearing maturity. He may still have a little more filling out to do, but he now looks like an adult Boxer. This can be the start of the trouble. Many first-time owners do not realize that adolescent dogs, like human teenagers, need to mature mentally as well as physically. The sex hormones kick in, and suddenly the world looks like a different place.

In most cases, a male dog will show more behavioral changes during adolescence than a female. A male is likely to be more assertive and more ready to challenge his status in the family. However, a female dog will also experience hormonal upheavals as she reaches sexual maturity, and she may be prone to moodiness and unsettled behavior.

The time at which these changes become apparent varies between individuals, but most Boxers will hit adolescence at around 11 or 12 months. Generally, a male is mentally mature at around 18 months to two years of age. Physically, he is not fully mature until around three years of age. Mentally, a bitch has usually matured by two years of age, which tends to coincide with the time she has reached physical maturity.

HANDLING ADOLESCENCE

The best way of handling an adolescent Boxer is to try to see things from his or her perspective. In the wild, a wolf pack tolerates youngsters until they become sexually mature. It is at this point that they become a threat to the

A male may be three years old before he reaches full maturity.

A female will generally be physically and mentally mature by two years of age.

established status as they challenge for a place in its hierarchy. The dog has been domesticated over many thousands of years, but this part of his inherited ancestral behavior remains intact. As he reaches maturity, a dog will try to gain a superior place in the family pack. During puppyhood he was content to be submissive, and this has been reinforced by training. But now he is not prepared to accept that your word is law. He questions your authority, and tests the limitations that are imposed on his behavior.

Do not throw your hands up in horror, fearing that your beloved Boxer has had a complete change in personality. This is a passing phase, and, if handled correctly, your dog will grow up into a well-balanced, well-behaved adult. Your dog is asking you questions: why should I come when I am called?; why should I sleep on the floor?; and why shouldn't I eat food left on the table? You must answer those questions firmly, fairly, and with total consistency. Your dog needs to know who is the boss, and, by reinforcing his early training, you are showing him that nothing has changed. You are the figure in authority that he must listen to in order to be accepted into the family pack.

A Boxer needs both his mind and his body to be exercised.

EXERCISING THE MIND

Training a puppy in basic obedience is one of the most enjoyable aspects of taking on a new dog. A Boxer puppy is quick to learn and, by the end of a 10-week training course, he will have mastered most of the straightforward exercises. You could be forgiven for thinking that your Boxer's education is complete and you can give up going to training classes. But that would be a big mistake for the following reasons.

- The Boxer is an intelligent breed and needs mental stimulation. A bored dog is likely to become deviant in his behavior.
- The social interaction with other dogs is of great benefit. Your Boxer learns how to behave acceptably with other dogs and he also learns that he must ignore them when he is working.
- Quality time at a training class, when you are concentrating solely on your Boxer, will help to improve your relationship with him. Ideally, training should continue throughout a

dog's life, but it will certainly be a great help in getting you through your dog's adolescence. You may well find that you get a taste for training and decide to have a go at one of the canine sports such as Competitive Obedience or Agility (see Chapter Five).

THE DOMINANT BOXER

The Boxer, and particularly the male Boxer, has a tendency to be dominant. This trait must be closely observed and monitored as your dog matures to ensure that he does not get the upper hand. Signs of dominant behavior include:

- Possessiveness of food or toys.
- Guarding personal space, often growling if someone comes too near to his bed.
- Pulling on the lead and lunging at people and other dogs he meets.
- Generally unresponsive to commands, and keen to follow his own agenda.

If you are concerned that your Boxer is becoming too dominant, it is advisable to seek the advice of a professional trainer or

A dominant Boxer may start to guard his personal space.

When you are playing, make sure you begin the game – and you decide when to finish it.

At the end of a game, you must take possession of the toy.

behaviorist who can help you to plan a program of dominance reduction. It is far better to nip this problem in the bud rather than to allow bad habits to become deeply ingrained.

Dominance reduction is a process of teaching your Boxer that he must back down on his claims of superiority and accept his inferior status in the family. There are many ways of putting this message across.

- Your Boxer must learn to wait every time you go through a door, or up and down stairs, and allow you to go first.
- Feed the family first, and then feed your Boxer.
- Do not feed your Boxer at family mealtimes.
- When you are playing with your Boxer, make sure you decide when to end the game – not him.
- If you are playing with a toy, take possession of the toy when the game is finished – do not let your Boxer run off with it.
- Do not allow your Boxer to sleep on the furniture.
- When your Boxer is eating, drop some treats into his bowl, then progress to taking the bowl from him for a few seconds. He needs to learn that you have control over his food.
- If your Boxer attempts to pull on the lead, come to a standstill and call your Boxer back to your side. You can use food treats as an incentive. If necessary, turn around so you are facing the opposite direction. Your Boxer must learn that pulling halts his progress. He can only move off again – which is what he wants to do – when he is back at your side.

This program should be backed up with regular training sessions, working at all the basic obedience exercises so that your Boxer respects your authority.

Never allow a dominance problem to get out of hand. At its worst, a Boxer that has been allowed to assert his own will can become aggressive, as well as uncooperative, and it may be too late to try to change his behavior. In these cases, professional help is highly recommended.

JUMPING UP

Boxers love jumping up, and while this is relatively harmless in a young puppy, it is no joke when a powerful adult tries to flatten you. It is a matter of particular concern where children are concerned – what starts as boisterous behavior can become both frightening and dangerous.

The best plan is to discourage any attempts to jump up right from the start. Use a command such as "Off," and gently put your puppy's front feet back on the ground. It is important to keep the command specifically for this situation, as a series of different commands – "Get down," "Down," "Get off," and so on – will only confuse him. Make a fuss of your puppy as soon as he is standing properly so that he learns that in this position he gets attention, rather than when he jumps up. Be 100 percent consistent when dealing with jumping up. It is all too easy to laugh at your puppy's clown-like behavior, but all you are doing is encouraging his bid to get attention in an unacceptable way.

Jumping up becomes a real problem when you are dealing with a big, powerful dog.

If your adolescent dog persists in jumping up, be very firm in your command "Off," and at the same time turn away from him. He is then getting the message loud and clear that he will be ignored if he jumps up. As soon as your Boxer has four feet on the ground, give him lots of praise.

When visitors come to the house, it is a good idea to put your Boxer on a lead, so that you can keep control of him. Command him to "Sit," and make sure he stays in this position while he is being greeted. The visitor could also be provided with a treat so that your dog is rewarded for staying in the Sit. If you have a very boisterous Boxer, try keeping him in the Down when he is being greeted. It is impossible for a dog to go from lying down to jumping up

A bored dog quickly becomes destructive.

in one movement, so you will have more time to act if your Boxer attempts to break position.

Make sure you reward your Boxer with verbal praise or a treat when he responds with correct, acceptable behavior. He will learn much more quickly if there is a positive aspect to his training rather than being constantly told off.

THE DESTRUCTIVE BOXER

The majority of dogs thrive on human company, but the Boxer craves attention and his behavior takes a downward spiral if he is left to his own devices. A bored dog quickly becomes a destructive dog, and if you are leaving your Boxer alone for too long, you only have yourself to blame.

Never leave your Boxer on his own for longer than three hours. If you ever have to do this, use the services of a dog-sitter or dog-walker so that your Boxer is not left unoccupied for too long.

The degree of damage your Boxer can inflict on your home depends on how freely

he can roam. If your Boxer is in a crate (see Crate-Training, page 29), he cannot chew the furniture or rip up a cushion. It is also helpful if you leave him with some boredom-busting toys, such a plastic cube with treats inside. Your Boxer will spend his time happily engaged in trying to get at the food and will have no time to think up any mischief.

BARKING

Boxers were bred to guard, and therefore a warning bark when strangers are approaching is only to be expected, and is generally appreciated. However, there are some Boxers who get a bit carried away, and continue barking long after your visitors have arrived. In most cases, this is simply a case of overexuberance, but bad habits quickly become ingrained, so you would be advised to take action.

The best way to stop a dog barking is to teach him to bark on command.

- Use a command, such as "Speak," and use it when your Boxer barks.
- Give him a reward, and distract his attention with a game so that he does not continue barking.
- Repeat this every time your dog barks, and he will learn to associate the command with what he is doing.
- You can then ask your Boxer to "Speak" on request.
- It is also a good idea to introduce a command, such as "Quiet," just before you

give the treat. Your Boxer will learn that he must stop barking in order to get his treat.

Be patient with this training exercise. It is well worth the effort to have a dog that is a useful guard – but not a nuisance. Remember, the Boxer is a high-spirited dog, and it is unfair to continually crush his enthusiasm. If your Boxer barks when he playing with another dog, or when he is first let off the lead – simply as a way of letting off steam – do not come down on him like a ton of bricks. Allow him the opportunity to run and bark, but then call him back to you and praise him quietly so that he does not become too excited.

SEPARATION ANXIETY

Destructive behavior may be a result of boredom, but it can also be linked to separation anxiety. The Boxer, with his great need for human company, may become very worried and concerned if he is left alone. The only way he can express his anxiety is by neurotic, inappropriate behavior. He may be destructive when he is left, his housebreaking may break down, or he may bark excessively.

From this it sounds as though the fault lies with the Boxer being unable to cope with periods of solitude. In fact, the owner is to blame for not teaching the dog that it is okay to be left for reasonable periods. When a puppy first arrives in his new home, he is usually swamped with attention. Owners take time off work, the children are always keen to play with the new arrival – and the puppy loves every

If a dog is not trained to spend time on his own, he may become very anxious.

minute of it. Then it is back to normal, and the puppy has to be left on his own for a period during the day. Instead of getting used to this gradually, the puppy goes from being surrounded by people to being abandoned. Needless to say, he is not impressed, and he shows his distress in deviant forms of behavior.

The secret is to wean your Boxer so that he learns to accept times on his own. This can start with as little as five or ten minutes a day, and gradually build up to longer periods of separation. If you have a crate, this will come in very useful as your puppy can go in his crate where he feels safe and secure. You can leave him with some boredom-busting toys (see page 25) which will help to keep his mind occupied and stop him from fretting. If a Boxer is brought up in this manner, he will learn that it is okay to be left and he will be content until you return.

A stairgate is a means of gradually accustoming your Boxer to coping on his own.

Coping With Anxiety

If your Boxer suffers from separation anxiety, there are several measures you can take.

- Buy a stairgate (used as a barrier for toddlers), and put it between two adjoining rooms. Go into one room, and leave your Boxer in the other room, with the door open and the stairgate in place. Your Boxer is on his own, but he can still see you. Gradually increase the amount of time your Boxer spends on his own before he is allowed to rejoin you.

- If you do not already have a crate, go out and buy one. A crate is seen as a safe haven, and your Boxer will be far more likely to settle if he feels secure. Take crate-training (see page 29) a step at a time, and gradually increase the amount of time your Boxer spends in his crate while you are still in the house.

- Make a few mock departures – picking up your car keys and putting on your coat – so that your Boxer does not get stressed seeing these "signs" of departure.

- When you go out, leave the radio playing at a low volume so your dog has the comfort of human voices.

- When you leave the house, make as little fuss as possible. Calmly put your Boxer in his crate and leave the house for a short period of around 10 minutes.

- When you return, do not greet your Boxer the second you get through the door. Leave him for a few minutes, and then calmly let him out of his crate.

It takes time and patience to re-educate a dog so that he does not experience anxiety when he is left. The best plan is to follow the advice above, and never allow your Boxer to become too dependent so that he feels he cannot cope on his own. If you are struggling with this problem, seek the advice of a professional trainer or behaviorist.

NEUTERING

If you are not planning to breed from your Boxer, you would be well advised to consider neutering your dog. This can have important health benefits, and, in certain cases, it can have a beneficial effect on behavioral problems.

Male Castration

Castration can prevent testicular cancer and balinitis (inflammation of the glans penis). It also offers a higher degree of protection against

Your vet will help you to decide when it is the best time to neuter.

prostate disorders in older dogs. If you have a dog with cryptorchidism (retained testicles), then castration is strongly advised, as the condition generates a far higher risk of developing testicular cancer.

The age at which to castrate your Boxer should be discussed with your vet. If you are neutering in an attempt to modify your dog's behavior, surgery must be carried out before your Boxer has learned behavior that may become habitual to him. If you wait until a male is older than two years and then castrate him in the hope that he will become less dominant or less aggressive toward other dogs, you are doomed to failure. A dog with this type of problem must be neutered as soon as the behavior becomes apparent, which is usually at 10 to 12 months as the dog enters adolescence.

Bitch Spaying

Neutering has many advantages for bitches that are to be kept solely as pets. Firstly and most importantly, it eliminates the problem of having to keep your bitch isolated for around 21 days twice a year when she comes into season. Some owners think this will be relatively easy to achieve, but you will find that, generally, your bitch is as eager to go and find the neighborhood dogs as they are to find her. There are far too many unwanted litters born every year to needlessly add to them.

In terms of health benefits, you take away the risk of your bitch suffering from pyometra (a pus-filled womb), and you minimize the risk of mammary tumors developing in later life. There is a belief that spaying can lead to obesity, but, if this does occur, it is easy to regulate with dietary control. There has also been a debate as to whether spaying can result in urinary incontinence in later life. However, there is no conclusive proof that spaying is the cause of the problem.

Ask your vet for advice as to when is the best age to spay. Some prefer to neuter before the first season; others recommend waiting until the bitch has had one season.

This is a big decision to make, for although the surgery is routine, there is always a slight risk when putting a dog, particularly a short-nosed breed like the Boxer, under general anesthetic.

If you are unsure as to whether to neuter your Boxer, talk to your vet who will help you to make the right decision.

CHAPTER FOUR

THE ADULT BOXER

After all the hard work of rearing a puppy and coping with adolescence, you are now rewarded with a full-grown Boxer that will, hopefully, be part of your family for the next 12 years or so. Boxers, perhaps more than any other breed, have a real need for human company, so make sure you let your dog join in with as many activities as possible.

It may seem a waste of time to take your Boxer for a short shopping trip – when he probably won't even get out of the car. But as far as your Boxer is concerned, this is a trip out with his people. He wants to be involved, so try to build a routine where he can share as much of your life as possible.

Boxers and children can get a great deal of fun playing with each other, as long as they both learn a sense of respect for each other. This must start while your Boxer is a puppy (see Chapter Two, page 34), for an exuberant adult Boxer can be quite a force to be reckoned with. However, if both dog and children are given the right education, the rewards are tremendous. The sweet, loving nature of a Boxer, combined with his clown-like sense of fun, make him a family companion that is second to none.

CARING FOR YOUR BOXER

Now that you have a beautiful, fully grown Boxer, your aim is to keep your dog happy and healthy for the rest of his life. Dogs are not difficult animals to look after, and, generally, Boxers are a fit, hardy breed, but it is important to find a regime that suits your own dog. You know him best, and you are responsible for giving him the care he needs.

COAT CARE

The Boxer is a very low maintenance dog in terms of coat care, and it is all too easy to neglect grooming because you do not have mats or tangles to deal with. However, a weekly grooming session has very important benefits.

FAMILY FAVORITES

Sharon Hannibal and her husband Rupert do not believe in doing things by halves. When they had three young children – Tony (nine), Ryan (six) and Joseph (four) – they took on their first Boxer, a six-month-old bitch called Fizz. They now have a family of five Boxers, and they also work as foster parents. At one time, they had eight Boxers and eight children living in the house . . .

"We used to own a pony and there was a Boxer at the stables," said Sharon. "This dog, Roxy, was so sweet and tolerant with the children that, when we decided to get a dog of our own, a Boxer was our first choice.

"I did everything you are not meant to do. I answered an advertisement in the local paper, and went and bought Fizz. The children were used to being around animals, and right from the start we taught them to respect Fizz. Joseph was still very young, but if he got too near her, we would say Gently, and he knew that he had to be careful.

"It was Ryan, who was then age six, who had the special relationship with Fizzy. Right from the start, she attached herself to him. In fact, when Ryan was naughty and I had to tell him off, I always made sure Fizzy was out of the room. She would never have done anything nasty, but she was very protective of him."

Sharon and Rupert took Fizzy to training classes, and soon they became involved in training for the show ring.

"Fizz was not really good enough to show, but we had a lot of fun with her, and we learned a lot," said Sharon. "It was enough to give us the bug, and soon we bought Ozmo as a show dog."

The Hannibals now have their own kennel prefix and they have bred five litters. Their current "pack" includes Fizzy (six), Ozmo (five), Dora (three), Minty (three), and Sidney (11 months). As the number of dogs multiplied, so did the children. Sharon and Rupert have been foster parents for the last ten years, and many children have become part of their family.

"At one time, we did mother and baby

The Hannibal house has always been full of Boxers and children!

fostering," said Sharon. "This is a scheme [arrangement] for single moms, and we looked after both mother and baby until they were ready to cope on their own. The first time we did this I was quite nervous about how the Boxers would react. They were used to children, but they had never met a baby. As it turned out, there was no need to worry. When the baby arrived home, the dogs came up as if to say: 'Let's have a look.' They were interested, but they were completely calm. Fizzy took her duties very seriously, and would lie down at the side of the baby carriage. If the baby's mother was not around, she would get very concerned and come and fetch one of us."

Sharon and Rupert now foster teenage boys, and they find the Boxers are a great help when it comes to settling the boys in.

"The social worker comes and fills in all the forms, and then the child is left with his new family," said Sharon. "It is a real wrench as they are leaving everything they have ever known. The last thing they want is us fussing over them. But the dogs seem to sense something, and they go and introduce themselves. It helps to break the ice, and it gives us all something to talk about."

Joseph, now age 11, is proving to be the dog enthusiast, and he loves going to all the shows. But the whole family joins in taking the Boxers for walks and looking after them.

"Boxers are marvelous with children," said Sharon. "They're like big kids themselves. They will play forever, and they are wonderfully tolerant. However, there are downsides, particularly with small children. The males, especially when they are adolescent, can be boisterous. Although they are a medium-sized breed, Boxers are powerful, and it is very easy for small children to get knocked over. Although it worked for me having Boxers with small children, I would say that generally they are better suited to slightly older kids who can withstand a bit of rough-and-tumble."

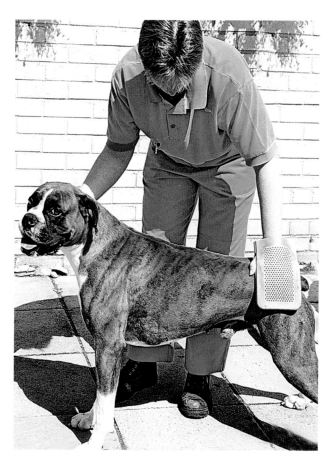

A rubber grooming mitt helps to drag out loose hairs.

• Grooming does more than tidy up the coat; it improves circulation, tones the muscles, and gets rid of dead hair.
• You are handling your Boxer and interacting with him, which will improve your relationship with him.
• A grooming session gives you the opportunity to give your Boxer a thorough check-over so that you can spot any sign of trouble at the earliest stage.

A rubber grooming mitt is best for the adult Boxer. This is made of heavy duty rubber, and is studded on one side. This helps to drag out any loose hairs, and also massages as you groom, toning up the muscles. As you work through your Boxer's coat, look out for anything unusual – such as a lump or a bump that you have not noticed before. There may be a small, bald patch, or you may find a sore area of skin. If you know what is normal for your Boxer, you will be swift to spot any changes. This is also a good time to check for any unwelcome parasites such as fleas (page 115) and ticks (page 117).

Ears

Check your Boxer's ears; the inside should be clean and fresh smelling. For some reason, Boxers seem prone to getting ear mites (see page 118). If your Boxer is scratching his ears and shaking his head, and the inside of the ears appears grubby and brown, he probably has ear mites. Your vet will prescribe suitable ear drops to treat this problem.

Eyes

The eyes should be bright and sparkling, with no sign of discharge. To freshen up, you can wipe around the eyes with a piece of cotton soaked in lukewarm water. Make sure you dry the area thoroughly.

Nose

Generally the nose should be damp, and there should be no discharge. Some dogs tend to have a drier nose; you should only be concerned if the nose appears cracked or crusty.

Teeth

The teeth should be clean, with no evidence of tartar accumulating. The gums should be pink and healthy, and your dog's breath should smell fresh. The teeth may need cleaning periodically, but, if you have practiced this with your Boxer when he was a puppy, it should not pose a problem.

If the ears need cleaning, make sure you do not probe into the ear canal.

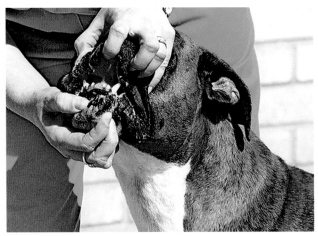

Check your dog's teeth to ensure there is no accumulation of tartar.

If the nails grow too long, they will need to be trimmed.

Feet and Nails

Check your Boxer's pads to make sure there are no cuts or cracks. The nails should be kept short. If your Boxer is not wearing them down naturally, you will need to clip them (see pages 32-33).

Bathing

Boxers are quite a fastidious breed and tend to keep themselves pretty clean. However, a bath will help to get rid of dead hair when your dog is shedding and it may be necessary if your Boxer finds something particularly smelly to roll in!

You can bathe your dog in a shower stall or in a tub, ideally fitted with a shower head. Make sure you have a rubber mat on the floor of the tub or shower stall to prevent slipping. Get your shampoo and towels assembled before summoning your Boxer, and then you should keep the spread of water to a minimum.

- Soak the dog's coat thoroughly with lukewarm water, and then apply the shampoo. (This should be a specially formulated canine shampoo.)
- Work the shampoo into a rich lather, making sure no shampoo gets near your Boxer's eyes or ears.
- Rinse thoroughly, making sure you remove all traces of the shampoo.
- Towel your Boxer dry, attempting to absorb most of the excess moisture before he is allowed to leave the bath.
- Your Boxer will be desperate to shake, so you can lead him out to the yard – but make sure he doesn't roll.
- If you have a blow dryer, put it on a low setting and you can dry your Boxer. Otherwise, just dry him with the towels.
- Finish off by grooming through the coat.

FEEDING

The golden rule is: once you have found a diet that suits your Boxer, stick to it. Boxers are not particularly fussy eaters, but they do not take kindly to change. A dog does not need variety in his diet, and, with Boxers in particular, it does more harm than good. It does not matter

Most Boxers thrive on a diet that is relatively low in protein.

whether you are feeding a complete diet, canned food, or fresh food, if your Boxer is doing well on it, do not attempt to change the status quo.

As a general rule, it is advisable to choose food that is fairly low in protein once your Boxer is fully grown. High-protein diets have led to behavioral problems in some dogs. Obesity must also be guarded against. The Boxer is a great actor, and will use his large doleful eyes and a mournful expression to prove how hungry he is . . . Do not be fooled. Your Boxer will stay far healthier if he is the correct weight for his size.

It is a good idea to ask your vet to weigh your Boxer once he is fully grown. The vet can advise you as to whether the dog is the correct weight and will be able to give you any advice on

feeding. It is also useful to have a note of your Boxer's "ideal" weight as part of his health record.

In many cases, food treats are used during training sessions, and, although you may not think you are giving very much food, you may well find that your Boxer is getting more than is good for him. The best plan is to work out how much you are giving your Boxer in the course of a training session, and then deduct it from his daily ration.

It is preferable to feed your Boxer two meals a day, rather than giving one big meal. This reduces the risk of bloat, which is a potentially life-threatening condition (see Chapter Seven). For the same reason, it is important not to feed your Boxer just before or just after strenuous exercise.

Bone of Contention

Dogs love to gnaw on bones and this is an excellent way of keeping the teeth clean and the gums healthy. It also provides pleasurable occupation for your dog. Make sure you only offer marrow bones, which cannot splinter. It is also essential that your Boxer is supervised when he has a bone, just in case of accidents.

Some dogs can get rather possessive when they have a bone. Do not make the mistake of thinking that "it is only natural" for a dog to guard his bone. This type of behavior is entirely out of place in a family dog, and you must put a stop to it at the very first sign of trouble.

• When you first give your Boxer a bone, sit with him and stroke him while he is gnawing

A bone provides occupation, as well as keeping the teeth clean, but make sure your Boxer is prepared to give up the bone when you say so.

it. Your Boxer must accept being handled while he is in possession of his "prize."

- From time to time, take the bone away. It may help if you swap the bone for a food treat or for a toy. Your Boxer must learn that he only has the bone when you allow it. It is within your power to take the bone away, and he must accept that this is your privilege.

- If your Boxer growls when you go near him, you must be extremely firm. Tell him "No" very firmly, and then command him to "Leave" his bone. As soon as he responds, reward him with a treat. Your Boxer must learn that he cannot "warn you off" with a growl. He must accept that the bone belongs to you – he can only have it when you say so.

Most Boxers are perfectly good-natured, and will never try to challenge your authority. But with some dogs, particularly a more dominant male, it is important to be able to read and react to their behavior so you can stop any trouble developing from the very earliest stage.

EXERCISE

Boxers are energetic dogs, and they need lots of exercise in order to stay fit and healthy. Rain or shine, your Boxer will need at least two 30-minute outings each day, with the opportunity to run off the lead so that he can stretch his limbs and burn off energy.

It has been found that Boxers who are deprived of exercise can develop behavioral problems. Some become difficult to manage, while others may become destructive. A bored dog is an unhappy animal. It is not altogether surprising that a Boxer in this situation will turn to crime.

Providing Variety

Exercise works on two levels. Firstly, it provides a means of stepping up the general level of physical activity. Secondly, it provides mental stimulation. When a dog is taken out, he is alert and interested in everything that is going on. He uses his canine sense to investigate new sights and smells, and his mind is fully occupied. For a lively, intelligent breed like the Boxer, exercise is a top priority and it is essential that owners share this view.

Try to make your outings as varied as possible. You will get fed up with walking the same route every day, and so will your Boxer.

EXERCISING YOUR BOXER

One of the great joys of owning an energetic Boxer is watching him running and playing – enjoying life to the fullest.

MAKING A SPLASH

*Swimming is an excellent form of exercise –
but make sure the environment is 100 percent safe.*

If you cannot go to new places, try to change the routine.

Keep your dog on lead for some parts of the walk, and keep changing the place where he is allowed to free-run. Some Boxers like to carry things, and they will enjoy holding a glove or a newspaper for part of the walk.

You can play retrieve games, and you can also break up the walk with a short training session if you can find a relatively distraction-free area. This will give your Boxer something to think about, and it will also help with overall control.

Swimming is an excellent form of exercise, and some Boxers really enjoy it. Make sure you find a safe stretch of water without currents. It is also important to find a shallow area where it is easy to get out of the water.

Do not overtire your dog, particularly if you are playing a retrieve game – some Boxers never know when they have had enough. Take a dry towel with you, and give your dog a good dry before returning home.

SECOND CHANCE

There are some Boxer owners who have never known their dog as a puppy. Adult Boxers are sometimes available from breeders, but the majority that are looking for homes come from rescue shelters. Unfortunately, there are all too many Boxers who end up in rescue, mostly through no fault of their own.

A Boxer may be given up for rehoming due to a change of situation, such as illness or a marriage breakup. In some cases,

a couple have decided to give up their dog when a baby is expected. Sadly, there are also a number of dogs who have been mismanaged by their owners, who then give up on them and pass them on for adoption.

It takes a lot of patience, understanding, and experience to take on a rescued dog. Even if there has been no history of problematic behavior, an adult dog is going to take time to adjust to a new home. Those who are very dedicated will give a second chance to a dog that has been mismanaged and will try to give him a fresh start.

Most commonly, the Boxers who come into rescue are adolescent males, generally aged between 18 months and two years. Frequently, a tendency to be dominant has been left unchecked, and the dog's behavior has deteriorated to the point where the owners can no longer control him. Another common problem is a Boxer who develops separation anxiety and becomes bored or destructive (see pages 51-52).

Staff at the rescue shelters will make a thorough assessment of every Boxer that is put up for rehoming, and dedicated staff work hard to sort out behavioral problems. In some cases, foster families take in a dog and try to re-educate and socialize him so that he has a better chance of being rehomed.

Despite this, a lot of hard work remains for the people who take on a rescued dog. It demands a very special commitment, but it can also bring a very special reward.

Penny Marsden-Draycott is an experienced dog person. She has worked in rescue kennels, and now works for a boarding kennel where she deals with a wide variety of breeds. But, for Penny, the Boxer is her all-time favorite. She has owned four Boxers – the latest is Doyle, a four-year-old brindle that came into rescue.

Doyle with Danielle and Chloe.

"I think everyone has a breed that means something special to them, and for me it is the Boxer," said Penny. "They are so loveable, I couldn't think of having any other breed."

Penny has two children, Danielle, age eight, and Chloe, age two, so she thought an adult dog would be a better choice than trying to cope with a puppy.

"Puppies are very time-consuming, and, as I work full-time, I didn't think I would be able to give one enough attention. I also did not want the children teasing a puppy," said Penny. "The problem with taking on a rescued dog is that, although you are missing out on the puppy phase, you do not know their background, and that could lead to problems."

When Doyle came into rescue, Penny was concerned that he might not work out as a family pet. "I was told that the previous owners couldn't control him, and he had knocked over their child. Of course I was worried because, no matter how much you love dogs, the children have got to come first."

She agreed to take Doyle home for one night to see how he reacted to the children.

"Right from the start, he was absolutely brilliant," said Penny. "My partner held the children, and I allowed Doyle to go up and meet them. He was perfectly calm and didn't make a fuss. I then gave each of the girls a bag of sweets, and Doyle let them eat them without trying to jump up. At the same time, I made sure the girls did not pull or poke at Doyle, and even the two-year-old understood that she must 'stroke gently.' We have never had any problems with him, so it just shows that a dog does deserve the benefit of the doubt. All the Boxers I have known before have been fairly boisterous, but Doyle is very laid-back."

Doyle settled into his new home in no time. He was reasonably well trained in his basic commands, and he had been taught that he couldn't go upstairs or go on the furniture.

"All that changed when he came to live with us," said Penny. "He lies on the sofa, and on my bed. He loves to be with us all the time."

Penny takes Doyle to work with her at the boarding kennels so he does not have to spend long periods on his own.

"He knows the routine, and is always ready to get in the car and come to work with me," said Penny. "As soon as he gets there, he heads for the kitchen because he knows his breakfast is waiting for him. He gets on fine with the other dogs, and never causes any trouble."

"We took him in for one night, and now I really couldn't hope for anything better," she said. "It is great to give a rescued dog another chance, but I do think you have to know what you are doing. You hear of Boxers coming into rescue because their owners cannot control them – they have bitten off more than they can chew. Boxers need time and attention, and, if you cannot give this to them, you may well end up in trouble."

THE AGING BOXER

With reasonable luck, your Boxer should live to a good age, and will remain healthy and active in his veteran years. Most Boxers live to at least 12 years of age, and many keep going for a couple of years beyond that.

Boxers are well known for staying young at heart, but it is important that you become aware of the changing needs of a dog as he gets older. When you are exercising your Boxer, let him dictate how far he wants to go, and let him go at his own pace. This is particularly important if you also have a younger dog who has more energy. Do not encourage your old dog to keep going. Let him have a quiet sniff or a chance to lie down while you have a hectic game of retrieve with the youngster. This will mean that both dogs get what they need. If you go for a walk in the rain, make sure you dry your Boxer when you get home. As he gets older, your dog will be inclined to be stiff, particularly if he gets wet or cold.

Boxers are prone to digestive upsets, so keep your aging Boxer on a plain, low-protein diet. There are complete diets which are specially formulated for veterans, and this may well suit your Boxer. Ask your vet for advice.

Bad breath is often a problem with elderly Boxers. The gums start to sag and food particles get trapped, resulting in foul-smelling breath and tooth decay. Keep the teeth clean with regular brushing, and, if your Boxer is still having problems, consult your vet. There is a simple procedure to lift the gums which has proved beneficial in many cases.

The veteran Boxer deserves special consideration.

Grooming sessions become even more important as a regular chance to check on your Boxer's general health. Take time to examine your dog thoroughly so that you can be aware of any changes at the very earliest stage. You may well find that your Boxer is not wearing his nails down naturally, and so you may need to trim them more regularly.

Take pride in your Boxer's appearance. The better he looks, the better he will feel.

THE FINAL PARTING

Sadly, there will come a time when your Boxer falls ill and the quality of his life is seriously affected. As a responsible, caring owner, you are faced with making the final decision to end your Boxer's days with dignity.

GOLDEN OLDIES

Jackie Drew, who has five Boxers of her own, has been involved with rescue work for nearly thirty years, and she has become known as the one who will always find room for an old dog.

"I love the oldies," she said. "There is something very special about the love a dog gives as he reaches the end of his life. They may not be so bouncy, but Boxers do not grow old gracefully. They really are perpetual puppies. My eldest dog, Pebbles, is now 13 years old, but she still pulls on the lead when we go out, and she is always on the go."

Inevitably, on many occasions, Jackie has had to face the trauma of losing dogs she has cared for.

"If you take on a dog, you must look after it to the very end," she said. "Sadly, that means you must be the one to decide when a life has lost its quality. It is never easy, but putting an end to suffering is something that we owe to our dogs."

"I think you can tell when a Boxer has had enough. The eyes go dull, and they seem to tell you that they are ready to go. The vet will come to my house and I cuddle the dog to say goodbye. The dog is completely unaware of what is happening – it is all very peaceful. My Boxers are always cremated, and we can choose whether to keep the ashes, or whether to bury them in the garden of rest by the crematorium.

"Unfortunately, many owners find it very hard to make the final decision. Often, they leave it too late because they cannot bear to let go. But I think we need to face up to the reality of what is happening. If a beloved dog is in pain and does not want to go on, we must respect his wishes. It is very painful for us, but it is a decision we must make selflessly, thinking about what is best for the dog rather than what is easier for us.

"I have talked to a lot of owners who are coping with bereavement, and they say it would not be right to have another dog. They think that it would be detrimental to the memory of the dog they have lost. But it is important to try to move beyond this. You have a loving home to offer to another Boxer, and it is a great shame to waste it. I always suggest that people choose a Boxer that looks very different, and then they can make a completely fresh start."

Enjoy your Boxer as he reaches the end of his life, but be prepared to make the right decision when the time comes.

CHAPTER FIVE

BROADENING HORIZONS

Throughout his history, the Boxer has shown that he is a first-class working dog, with the intelligence to take on new tasks, and the willingness to always do his best. If you have chosen a Boxer as your preferred breed, you will be aware of his need to be mentally challenged. If you neglect this side of his character, you will be faced with a bored animal that may well become badly behaved. It is in your interest to harness your Boxer's willingness to work, and to go out and have fun with him.

CANINE GOOD CITIZEN

The "Good Citizen" program is an excellent starting point if you want to expand on your dog's initial puppy training. The American Kennel Club's Canine Good Citizen Program and the British Kennel Club's Good Citizen Dog Scheme encourage responsible pet ownership and educate dog owners about the benefits of having a well-behaved pet.

For the boisterous Boxer, a program of early training and socialization is essential, and the Good Citizen tests give you something to aim for. The tasks that are set are not challenging; they are designed to produce well-mannered canine citizens. Dogs are

The intelligent Boxer will enjoy training sessions, particularly if you intersperse work and play.

examined on behaving well in everyday situations, including:

- Accepting handling and grooming
- Responding to basic obedience commands
- Meeting another dog
- Walking on a loose lead in a controlled manner
- Walking confidently through a crowd of people
- Being approached and petted by a stranger.

If your Boxer needs to polish up his skills, see Chapter Two. There are many participating training clubs in the United Kingdom and the United States where you can enroll to prepare your dog for the tests. To find out more information on the programs, contact your national Kennel Club.

AGILITY

Agility is a great favorite with dogs and owners alike. It is one of the sports where you can really see a dog's enjoyment – and the level of fitness that is required is good for all concerned!

In Agility, the dog must tackle a series of obstacles in the correct order, within a set time, and with no faults. The winning dog is the one that completes a clear round in the fastest time. A degree of basic obedience is required before starting. Your dog should be well-behaved around other dogs, and you should have basic control over him, so that he won't just run off to play with one of his fellow pupils as soon as he is let off the lead.

Dogs must be fully grown before attempting Agility, or they could damage vulnerable bones and joints. The U.K. Kennel Club excludes any dog under 18 months from competing; the American Kennel Club has a lower age limit of 12 months.

Once you believe your Boxer is ready for training, join a local Agility club. This is the best place to learn all the techniques, to get your dog used to performing around other dogs, and to pick up useful training tips.

JUMPING FOR JOY

Margie Burton and her Boxer Tom, who are based in California, had one go at Agility – and they were both hooked! Now Margie is working with her youngster, Chad, who is also showing a real liking for the sport.

"I joined an Obedience training club to meet more doggie folks, and for the camaraderie and encouragement," said Margie. "I met a lady who raised Dobermans, and she encouraged me to come to Agility classes. I did, and both Tom and I loved it. Unlike Obedience Trials, where you are not supposed to speak to your dog except to issue a command, in Agility we can talk to our dogs all we want. This really appealed to me as I believe in verbal praise for any task well done – and in the instant reinforcement for a completed task."

Margie believes that Boxers are well suited to Agility, both in terms of temperament and conformation. "I feel a compact, muscular body is ideal for Agility," she said.

JUMPING FOR JOY

Tackling the tunnel.

"I would particularly encourage those who may not have a 'standard-sized' Boxer to train in this sport. My dog Tommy is on the smaller side, about 22.5 inches tall, but he can really sail over those jumps. As to temperament, most Boxers love to please, and giving instant verbal praise lets them know they are doing well.

"Most Boxers get bored easily, so the variety of the obstacles and course makes this an ideal Boxer sport. It seems that Boxers have an in-built 'play gene,' and so Agility really appeals to them. Most of them love the new game of going over jumps and through tunnels. I also find that Agility gives those somewhat shyer dogs a new sense of confidence and boldness. It challenges them to really think, to reason, if you will, on how to follow directions and keep track of their handler."

There is the small matter of getting your Boxer to concentrate on the business at hand. "For me, the biggest problem has been keeping Tommy from racing off-course to go visit some cute little furry Pom, or other small dog with a waving tail!" said Margie.

"The other things to deal with include heat (both dog and handler), and my own lack of fitness in running a long course. As far as Tom is concerned, I have had to work at keeping his

attention and enthusiasm throughout a long day. These are challenges that can be ongoing. It is also important to appreciate that a dog may simply decide that today is not his day to shine. He may decide that little Terrier over there is much more interesting than a series of jumps, or that he is just too hot and tired to show any pizzazz."

Margie believes there is no substitute for strong, basic obedience training when you and your Boxer first start in Agility. "Having a dog that responds quickly to commands such as 'Come,' 'Wait,' 'Over,' and 'Heel' is very helpful," she said. "More commands can be added as each obstacle is learned. You also need to work on your timing so that you give prompt verbal rewards when a dog has done well.

"There is one other important factor to consider: do not start your dog jumping until the growth plates in his legs have stopped growing. Agility can be stressful to young, undeveloped bodies. Care should be taken not to stress the growing bones of puppies. They can, however, learn to go between the poles and to go through tunnels without danger to the growing bones."

Margie says that she has found the weaving poles the hardest obstacle to train. "Going over a jump is fun and makes sense, going up the

Over the hurdles.

JUMPING FOR JOY

Negotiating the dog-walk.

dog-walk is easy and fun . . . but those darn weave poles, whatever in the world are they for? The best way to teach weaves is to start with just two or three poles. Once the dog gets the hang of going between them, we add a couple more. Keep your dog on lead and show him where, and how, to go. Give big praise for any progress."

Although Boxers are quick learners, Margie advises patience when training for Agility. "Each obstacle presents its own challenge for a dog to learn, but once they get the hang of it, they are so proud of themselves. Each obstacle should be learned more or less at the dog's pace. If a dog seems hesitant to go up, or over, the A-frame, for example, help him up, and keep a constant hold on the collar. Let him take his time in coming down, still holding the collar, and encourage him all the way. Generally, it only takes one or two times of 'helping' before the dog will do the obstacle with flair."

Margie well remembers the time when Tom was ready to tackle the A-frame on his own. "Tommy had recently conquered the mighty A-frame, and he was enjoying his new confidence," she said. "Away we went, through the course, and as we came to the A-frame I called out: 'Up.' Tommy raced to the top of the A-frame – and there he stood, tall, handsome, smart, admiring the view. I could just hear him thinking . . . 'my,

look at those birds over there, and say, the neighbors actually have a cat . . . wow, I didn't know that! Hey, I can see clear over the fence, and look at that, a plane overhead . . . What? Come down, you say?' There I stood, patiently waiting at the foot of the A-frame while Tom stayed where he was, totally entranced with his new perspective on the world!"

Margie and Tom have had many high spots in their Agility career, but they have also had a few moments they would rather forget . . .

"At our first trial, Tom was far more interested in who had gone over the course before him. He felt it was of utmost importance that others should know that he had passed this way too . . . Therefore, he dutifully marked several of the obstacles before we got dismissed from the course – not to mention that we had, by now, run way over the allotted time allowance. Well, Tom had fun anyway!"

Margie's big ambition is to compete at the ABC Nationals. But she is keeping her feet firmly on the ground. "Only time will tell how far we can go," she said. "In the meantime, I would like to find a foolproof way to keep my Boxer's attention on me instead of on those little furry things around the ring that yap like a squeaky toy!"

Steady on the seesaw.

A Group Stay: The Boxer can be trained to a high level of obedience – but it is not a test for the faint-hearted.

FLYBALL

Flyball is best described as a canine relay race. Two teams compete against each other on two identical tracks, each 51 feet long (15.5 meters). Each dog must leap the four hurdles, trigger a box to release a ball which the dog must catch, and then return to the starting/finishing line before the next dog can start.

If a ball is dropped, or a hurdle is knocked, it is deemed a fault, and the culprit must run the course again after the last member of the team has run. The team that completes in the fastest time wins.

Flyball is incredibly popular in the United States and the United Kingdom. It is fairly simple to teach, but is more difficult to be very good at, as the standard of the top teams is very high – America, Canada, and the United Kingdom have all achieved team times under 17 seconds.

Because of his size, the Boxer is not as naturally agile as, for example, the Border Collie or Working Collie. The Boxer is a dedicated worker, and many have overcome their slight physical disadvantage, working that little bit harder, to compete in teams around the world.

COMPETITIVE OBEDIENCE

The Boxer is an intelligent, biddable breed, but for most, the challenge of training a Boxer in Competitive Obedience is daunting. The exuberant nature of a Boxer poses huge problems when it comes to the precision required in this canine discipline. However, there are those that have bucked the trend, and become successful in this sphere.

The exercises in Competitive Obedience/Obedience Trials vary slightly depending on where you are competing, but the basics are as follows.

Heelwork: Your dog is required to walk beside you on your left side, both on and off the lead, and to remain close (neither forward nor behind, but with his head level with your knee) whatever direction you take. Once your Boxer can walk in the correct position, you need to introduce changes of pace, and changes of direction.

Recall: This exercise becomes increasingly difficult as you advance in training. A simple, "novice" Recall involves putting your Boxer in the Sit, leaving him, and calling him in. The dog must sit in the Present position, and then finish by coming to the left-hand side of his handler. A more complicated Recall is done with the handler on the move, calling the dog in to his side.

Retrieve: The dog must retrieve a dumbbell (in the advanced classes, any object chosen by the judge) thrown by the handler. Your Boxer must wait until he is given the command to "Fetch." He must pick up the dumbbell cleanly and then return and sit in front of the handler to present it, before returning to the handler's side.

Send Away: This is where the dog is sent in a direction indicated by the judge, drops down at the owner's command, and is recalled in a certain direction (again, indicated by the judge).

Scent discrimination: A series of cloths are laid out, and the Boxer must pick out the cloth with the judge's scent. In advanced classes, "decoy" scented cloths are also included to make the task more difficult.

Agility: In the U.S., Obedience Trials include an Agility section, which includes the obstacles used in the U.K. Working Trials (see below).

TUNING INTO THE BOXER MIND

Some people cannot resist a challenge, and that certainly includes those who train their Boxers to compete in Obedience Trials. Karla Spitzer has proved all the critics wrong, and has gone to the very top of the tree with her three Boxers, Cleo, Harpo, and Kosmo. Her outstanding achievement is with Harpo who is, to date, the world's only male Boxer to be awarded the Utility Dog Excellent title.

Karla grew up with dogs, mostly herding breeds such as Border Collies, German Shepherd Dogs, and Rough Collies, but her life changed when she acquired her first Boxer, Cleo, 11 years ago.

"I was first attracted to Boxers because they are just so interesting looking," she said. "They are so athletic and smart. They look as though they have this big, huge secret. I also found that they are way more interested in people than most of the herding dogs. They are certainly one of the most intelligent breeds I have worked with – which can be a mixed blessing."

When Karla got to know the breed, she became fascinated by the seeming contradictions in the Boxer temperament.

"I find them playful, yet cautious," she said. "They are intelligent with a wonderful sense of humor. They are incredibly loyal about the things that count (in their minds), yet pretty laissez-faire about life in general. They can be a challenge because of their intelligence. Without training and things to think about, they can revert to being very territorial and fairly dominant. They, like many breeds, need to work (or at least be clear about the rules), and they must have a lot of interaction with humans in order to be canine good citizens.

"Cleo, our first Boxer puppy, was so awful that I knew we needed more help and structure. She was nothing like the herding breed puppies I grew up with. She was trouble (the puppy from hell). In fact, she was not entirely atypical of most Boxer puppies! By the time she was about a year old, we had also acquired Harpo, who was then about 10 weeks old. I found an AKC Obedience judge, Shirley Indelicato, who ran training classes. At three months, Harpo joined her puppy class, and Cleo (then about 16 months old) was entered

Jacquet's Cello Giocoso CGC: A sweet, whimsical Boxer who has won two Best of Breed in conformation.

for the basic class. Shirley didn't say much about Cleo, but she reckoned that Harpo "could be good in obedience."

"At this time, I was volunteering at an all-breed shelter, working with the difficult dogs. I had worked with difficult dogs in the past with considerable success, and I found that I could pretty easily train the 'basics' of walking on lead without pulling too much, the sits and downs, etc. I also saw how incredibly bonded the dogs were with their owners in the Obedience classes, and I sort of put two and two together. I love working with dogs, and seeing all the untrained dogs that ended up in rescue, I realized that training a dog in Competitive Obedience would solve many behavioral problems before they got out of hand. Part of my intent also was to live peacefully in an urban area with my dogs whose behavior had to be appropriate and manageable."

Karla's ambitions were modest to begin with, but then a big challenge came her way.

"I was told that I would never get an Obedience title on an intact (non-neutered) male Boxer, so the race was on. I simply couldn't resist that challenge. Not only did I get that title (what they had really meant was the lowest level title, the CD or Companion Dog title), but Harpo went on to become the world's only Boxer male Utility Dog

Excellent, and the only male Boxer to be invited to the AKC Obedience Invitational (all while remaining intact).

"He's a pretty grand kind of guy, and has managed his hormones very well, which is something that not all dogs of any breed can do. And he's still going (he has just gone High in Trial and Senior Veterans Sweeps winner at the Boxer Club of San Fernando Valley Specialty)."

IMAGINATIVE THINKING

Karla is the first to admit that training Boxers to this level is not always easy, but she believes it is a matter of finding the training methods that are best suited to the breed.

"Boxers have not been a popular Obedience breed in the U.S. for at least 30 years. When a breed becomes popular in this discipline, it generally follows a course of a competitor becoming very successful with a specific breed, and then training others within the breed to be equally successful. At the moment, Border Collies, Australian Shepherds, and Golden Retrievers are very popular Obedience competition dogs. The breeds that have been pretty popular in the recent past are Shetland Sheepdogs and Poodles.

"The result of this is that current training

Harpo The Marker UDX: Boxers love jumping, and this exercise comes easily to them.

methods are designed to be fairly breed-specific. While it is true that all breeds are 'canines,' I feel that there is a different learning curve in many breeds. In the classes that I took with Harpo, the retrieving and herding breeds often seemed to get things more quickly. They seemed to need more repetition, yet their learning curves seemed to rise rapidly and steadily. Harpo and my other Boxers seemed to have learning curves that were more of a flat line and then a spike – not always encouraging, to say the least. However, once they really learned what they needed, they required less repetition to retain what they had learned."

THINKING TIME

"I think that this may be a working dog tendency. A Boxer may seem slow to commit to new behaviors at times, but I think it is not so much that the dog is stubborn, but that he wants to be very, very sure of what he is doing before repeating a behavior. Personally, I don't think that this is such a bad thing. Even though progress may not be so rapid, once a Boxer has learned something, he will surpass many of his classmates. Many instructors who have not worked with Boxers have seen this as stubbornness, and felt the breed needed harsher training. In fact, what they benefit from is more clarity in training."

Some of the exercises in Competitive Obedience come more naturally to Boxers than others.

"I think that mine like jumping the best," said Karla. "We have trained a motivational jump in the ring for both Obedience and Conformation. The second most enjoyable exercise for my dogs is scenting. That can be tracking, finding things that are hidden in the house, or getting the correct scent articles in the ring. Scenting seems to be something that Boxers are very good at.

"Harpo has an excellent nose. He knows where the correct scented article is in most cases (unless it's raining or really windy) long before he gets to the article pile. He also likes to check out the crowd, so he has fooled many a judge into thinking he's working by going around and around the pile (even though I can tell he knows where the right one is), simply to look at the crowd!"

Inevitably, there is one exercise that Karla dreads in the ring.

"Quite embarrassingly, for me it's basic heeling," she said. "Yep, I know my Boxers should easily and readily be able to walk at my side with attention. But, despite the fact that I could have walked to the moon and back with several of my Boxers in training, my guys seem to think that they should keep an eye on the crowd, and anything going on outside the ring, rather than gazing at me with that rapt Border Collie attention. I think this is, again, their guarding/working tendency coming out. Or it could be that Boxers are plain nosy, and simply want to know what is going on around them. Although I love to train, maybe I don't take competition, as such, quite as seriously as I should. That said, we aren't horrible (most of the time), but there are better Boxer heeling teams than me and my Boxers."

GOING SOLO

There was one memorable occasion when Harpo decided to take charge of the heeling exercise in the ring.

"I had broken a toe, and I was showing Harpo in 'Open A,'" said Karla. "I could sense that Harpo knew there was something was wrong with me. When we got to the heelwork, the judge used the same heeling pattern as she had used in the novice ring prior to our class. Harpo had watched this, so when the judge said 'forward,' Harpo trotted out briskly, and before I could say anything, he pretty much did the whole heeling pattern with halts, turns, and all. He gave me a look as if he was saying to me, 'I know your toe hurts, so you stay right there – I can do this.' Well, the AKC doesn't see things in quite the same way, and we were zeroed on heeling, but you've got to give the guy credit!

"That same day, when the judge said, 'throw your dumbbell over the high jump,' Harpo took off and waited on the other side for it. People were falling off their chairs laughing as he carefully peered at the jump, waiting patiently. I was pretty nonplussed by now, and, as I didn't want to brain him with his heavy dumbbell, I threw it off to the side. He retrieved it, lined himself neatly up to the jumps and brought it back. He had anticipated the drop as well (not an uncommon mistake), so the only thing he qualified on was the broad jump. The judge threw her pen and clipboard in the air, and said: 'he clearly knows what to do, but!'

Harpo retrieving a scent article, which constitutes one of the Utility exercises. He is ten years old – and still competing.

"Before going into the ring, my constant reminder to Harpo from that day forward is: 'Don't help me – just do as I say!'"

Karla believes that building a successful partnership with your Boxer starts at the first moment when you go out and choose a puppy.

"Try, if you can, to meet the parents of the pup, and make sure they have passed all the relevant health checks," she said.

"Never buy a pup who has been taken from the litter earlier than eight weeks, and never buy a pup from a puppy store. Work hard at early and frequent socialization, or go to puppy socialization classes. It is also important to bear in mind that while most Boxers (especially the males) are not necessarily looking for a fight, most will not back down. Therefore, the golden rule is not to let your Boxers fight at all."

Karla believes that a puppy is ready for training as soon as he arrives in his new home.

▶

Harpo SocialGrace d'Jaquet (left) and Harpo's SocialCharm d'Jaquet. Training should start early, but it should be kept light-hearted.

"I start all my dogs with some basics as early as possible, usually no later than 8 to 12 weeks," she said. "I like to keep it fun and light in tone. Puppies are learning so much that it is so important in their personal (temperamental) development not to put on a lot of pressure. I find fun, motivational training, that is very clear, is the best ticket to a happy, working Boxer. Clicker training can be one very clear method, but there are others that simply involve laying a good groundwork that may be equally as good."

Karla has had many high spots in her competitive career, but there are a few moments that have a special value.

"I remember every title on Cleo, Harpo, Kosmo, and now Helio, but most particularly Harpo's UD and UDX. That first UDX leg was big, as was the next nine (it takes 10 qualifying legs in both Open and Utility B for a UDX). His Highs in Trial, mostly at Specialties, and High Combined (highest combined score from the open and utility classes) were special. His High Combined from the Obedience Club of San Diego County was very special. But probably the most special was the day I got the written invitation from the American Kennel Club for the 2000 Obedience Invitational. I was so proud of Harpo that day. He has been such a very, very great dog."

LOOKING AHEAD

Despite her huge success in Obedience, Karla still has a few ambitions left.

"I keep training for tracking, and would love to actually be able to pass a tracking test," she said. "I am working with my younger dogs to see if I can get an Obedience Trial Championship, and a breed Championship. To date, I have put two Best of Breeds on my three-year-old, Cello, which is very hard to do in this country especially for an owner-handler with a bitch."

For those starting out in Competitive Obedience, she recommends finding a good motivational trainer – with a sense of humor, particularly if they have never trained Boxers before. But she adds an important note of caution:

"Remember that no matter what you do in training or in trials or tests, your Boxer remains your very good friend. Regardless of the result on the day, he will be coming back to a home where he is loved and appreciated."

THE VERSATILE BOXER

Tracy Hendrickson has proved the amazing versatility of the Boxer with her Sunchase team of dogs, who have won more than 100 working dog titles. She is the first to admit that training Boxers is not easy.

"If anyone asked my advice about training Boxers in Obedience, I would say, if you really want to be competitive, get a Golden Retriever! If you just want to have fun and be humored, get a Boxer! You can train four Goldens in the time it takes to train one Boxer."

Tracy has certainly been rewarded for all the effort she has put into training her dogs, and she can boast some fantastic achievements. Her titled dogs include: Ch. Sunchase Fashionably Late U-ATCH, U-AGI, U-AGII, U-CD, U-CDX, INT'L, CD, BDA CD, DX, NA, NAJ, CGC, TDI, VCC, VCCX, VO, Sunchase's Caught Peeking, U-CD, CD, CGC, TDI, TT, and Sunchase's Zero To Hero, U-ATCH, U-AGI, U-AGII, U-CD, BDA CH, AM CH, INT'L CH, CD, BDA CD, TDI, CGC, BH, AD, VCC, VCCX.

Tracy says: "Training a Boxer needs to be started at an early age in order for him to be molded into a treasured pet. Puppy classes are the best for molding future positive behavior patterns. However, older dogs can still learn and can often be more focused."

The Boxer that Tracy is most proud of is Sunchase Suicide Blonde, U-ATCHX, U-AGI, U-AGII, U-CD, U-CDX, U-UD, U-CH,

The Sunchase team of working dogs..

AM/CAN/BDA Ch. Sunchase
Suicide Blonde: The true all-
rounder who holds 27 titles.

AM/CAN/BDA CH, AM/CAN/BDA CD, CDX, UD, NA, NAJ, OA, OAJ, TT, TDI, CGC, BH, AD, VCC, VCCX, VO, H.I.C.

Tracy sees Chili, who holds a grand total of 27 titles, as the ultimate example of a working dog. She has acquired multiple high in trial awards as well as having dozens of perfect scores in Agility. She has been an enthusiastic competitor in the Obedience ring and obtained the coveted Dog World award for consistently high scores. What is the secret of her success?

"Boxers learn fast, but get bored easily," says Tracy. "You have to make yourself interesting to the Boxer you are training.

"This will help keep his attention and motivate him to keep on working. Repetitive training will only bore a Boxer. Keep training

sessions short until he is willing to focus for longer periods of time."

Chili is not only a rare combination of brains and beauty, she also has a wonderful temperament, and is trained as a therapy dog. Her work does not stop there, however. Chili is one of the many Sunchase dogs who is used regularly as a blood donor.

It is hard to believe that Tracy has any ambitions left for her kennel of working dogs, but she is determined to train an Obedience Trials Champion – as there has only been one to date in the Boxer breed.

"I would also like to help people to communicate with, and understand their Boxers from the start. This would help to prevent abuse and abandonment of the breed," she said.

THE SUNCHASE TEAM IN ACTION

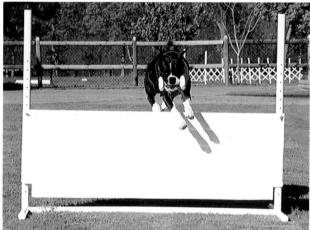

WORKING TRIALS/TRACKING

In the United Kingdom, Working Trials involves Tracking, Agility, and Obedience. It tests the dog's accuracy, concentration, temperament, and strength. There are not many Boxers competing in this discipline, but those who have become involved have proved very successful.

In the United States, many of the Working Trials skills are tested in Competitive Obedience (e.g., heeling on and off lead, Sit and Down exercises, retrieving a dumbbell over a solid high jump, broad jump over a series of low wooden hurdles, and so on). For this reason, the Working Trials titles of Companion Dog, Companion Dog Excellent, and Utility Dog are also used in U.S. Obedience (with the addition of Obedience Trials Champion – OTCh.). In the United States, the tracking element is a separate sport and has its own titles (see below).

CHANNELING THE BOXER BOUNCE

Carry On Katie CDex, UDex (left) and Witherford Amber Brown UDex, WDex.

Ruth Perrett became involved with Boxers nearly 30 years ago, first working in a show kennel, and then taking over the famous Bockendon prefix in 1949. Her Boxers are show-quality animals who are successful in the ring, but she has also taken on the challenge of stretching their minds and training them in the demanding discipline of Working Trials.

"To begin with I just wanted to work with dogs, but when I got to know Boxers, I soon became addicted to the breed," she said. "Although Boxers are very much in the minority in Working Trials, I think they are ideally suited to this type of work. They are so willing to please, and so curious about everything that is going on. All their bounce and energy are channeled into an athletic body, and, to me, they are natural working dogs."

Ruth believes that the variety of tasks in Working Trials – Obedience, Agility, and Tracking – suits the Boxer temperament more than the

CHANNELING THE BOXER BOUNCE

Caligula of Bockendon CDex, UDex, WDex, TD open.

more rigid structure of Competitive Obedience.

"Boxers hate repetition," she said. "You teach a Boxer to do something, and then you leave it, returning to the task only when you need to. Breeds such as Border Collies and German Shepherd Dogs thrive on a seemingly limitless workload, but Boxers do not see the point of that. They have a tremendous memory, and if you teach a lesson well, it will remain in the repertoire without needing to practice it continuously."

Ruth has trained two Boxers in Working Trials: Bockendon Come On Katie CDex, UDex, Witherford Amber Brown UDex, WDex, and she bred Caligula Of Bockendon CDex, UDex, WDex, TD trained by Ray Rowarth, who has competed in open TD. She found Tracking the most rewarding discipline to teach.

"There is a misconception that a flat-faced breed, such as the Boxer, will not have a good nose," she said. "In fact, they are terrific trackers. There is no greater feeling than going to the start of a track when you have no idea where the trail goes, or where the articles are located, and just allowing your dog to take the lead."

Ruth has enjoyed many high spots in her career, but she has also had the occasional embarrassing moment when the irrepressible Boxer character came to the fore.

"I was sending Amber Brown out to do a Sendaway, which was positioned at a distance of about 100 yards, alongside a stone wall. Amber went off like a shot from a gun – and leapt straight over the stone wall!

"Boxers always have their own agenda. You can train something, but you cannot guarantee they are going to produce it on cue."

Ruth's training is entirely reward-based, and she finds that toys are a greater source of motivation than food. She also warns that a highly trained Boxer is quite a demanding animal.

"If you wake up their working instincts, they really want the stimulation of being given things to do. You need to keep working with them."

Ruth now has a young bitch in her kennel, Bockendon Gift Of The Gab, who she hopes will carry on the kennel's Working Trials tradition. "She certainly looks the part; we will just have to see how things turn out," she said.

Working Trial Titles

In Working Trials, there are several different levels, each one testing the handler's control, and the dog's agility and nosework. The levels get progressively more difficult. For example, the Companion Dog (CD) Stake involves:

• Heeling on and off leash
• Recall to handler
• Sending the dog away
• Two-minute Sit
• 10-minute Down
• Clear jump
• Long jump
• Scale, Stay, Recall
• Retrieving a dumbbell
• Elementary search.

In U.S. Obedience many of these skills are tested in both CD and CDX.

By the time you have passed Companion Dog, worked through Utility Dog (UD), Working Dog (WD) and Tracking Dog, you come to the ultimate test, Patrol Dog (PD), which not only tests the dog's advanced control, agility, and nosework, but also involves a category on searching for criminals:

• Quartering the ground
• Test of courage
• Search and escort
• Recall from criminal
• Pursuit and detention of criminal.

To achieve such a high level of control, you must attend a Working Trials club for specialist training.

U.S. Tracking Titles

The three tracking titles each test the dog's ability to identify and follow a human scent. These skills are used every day by life-saving rescue dogs all over the world.

Tracking Dogs (TD): To earn his TD, a dog needs to follow a recent track (laid thirty minutes to two hours previously). The track of 440 to 500 yards will involve three to five turns. The dog is also expected to retrieve or indicate the location of an article (glove or wallet).

Tracking Dog Excellent (TDX)

A TDX involves following an older track (laid three to five hours previously). The track is longer (800 to 1000 yards) and more turns are involved (five to seven). The dog should retrieve or indicate four different articles.

Variable Surface Tracking (VST)

To earn his VST a dog must follow a 600- to 800-yard track laid three to five hours previously. It may take him down a street, through a building, and through other typical urban areas. Four to eight turns are involved, and four items should be found.

SECURITY WORK

In the early days of his development, the Boxer was highly prized for his work with the armed services. Today, the breed is rarely used for police and security work – with a few notable exceptions.

DOGS WITH A MISSION

Cathy Markos and husband, George, who are based in Mindoro, Wisconsin, were brought together by Boxers, and now their lives revolve around the breed. An interest in training Boxers in Tracking and personal protection has led to dazzling success in competition, and, even more importantly, in the field of drug detection. The historic role of the Boxer as a police dog has been revived, and there is now a growing band of enthusiasts who appreciate this very special aspect of the breed.

"George acquired his first Boxer, a striking, brindle male named Rebel, in 1986," said Cathy. "He was interested in finding a dog that could be trained in personal protection work and also for Schutzhund competition. After a year-long search, he found Rebel (Reward's Rebel Rouser, SchH1), whose father was a German import, and mother an American show Champion. George loved the powerful look of the breed, and found the character and personality of the breed to be perfect for him.

"This is where I come into the story. I am a dog trainer by profession, and own a training center in Wisconsin. George came to me for assistance in continuing his training with Rebel. I fell in love with the breed (and with George), and we've been together since. We always joke that George married me so he would not have to pay for training lessons anymore!

"George and I are now both Special Deputies for the Jackson County Sheriff's Department. We train the county's K9 (a German Shepherd we imported and trained for them), and we also are available to be called out with our own dogs. This is usually for bigger drug searches when a number of buildings or areas need to be investigated, rather than for smaller traffic stops. We are often called to prisons and schools, and we are also available to do searches for missing persons or fugitives. But the drug work is where we are most needed.

George Markos and Reward's Rebel Rouser SchH1 during an early morning Tracking session.

SCHUTZHUND

"Tracking is an integral part of Schutzhund, which is made up of three separate phases, Tracking, Obedience, and Protection work. Each is worth 100 points of the total 300 point score, so it is important that the dog be well versed and reliable in tracking. Since Schutzhund was the dog sport we wanted to work in, it was necessary to learn all we could about tracking.

"Rebel was the first Boxer we tracked with, and it was difficult right from the start. Of course, we were 'newbies' to Tracking, which did not help matters, and the Schutzhund trainers we worked with had no experience whatsoever with Boxers – they were used to German Shepherd Dogs. It was a very frustrating experience for us.

"We began to contact as many people as we could around the country and in Germany who had experience with working Boxers, and we slowly developed methods which worked, primarily manipulating the food drive of the dogs. Rebel did eventually get the idea, but he was never a truly reliable tracker. Our subsequent dogs were easier."

DOGS WITH A MISSION

Axel von Bachbett BH, SchH1, VCCX reacts to the threatening "bad guy" by gripping the padded sleeve. He must release his grip as soon as the man stops fighting.

Axel von Bachbett retrieves over a meter-high jump, which is part of the Schutzhund Obedience phase.

Axel von Bachbett does a "hold and bark" exercise during the Schutzhund Protection phase. The dog may not touch the "bad guy" during this phase; he must hold him at bay.

Grobi vom Hafen BH SchH1, FH2, ZTP, AD, O-VCCX: The first Boxer in North America to earn the highest Tracking title in Schutzhund, the FH2.

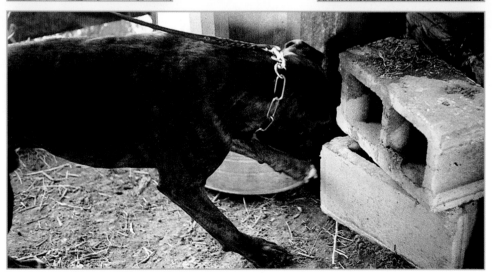

Police K9 Ivo vom Hafen BH, SchH3, IPO3, ZTP, O-VCCX gives a scratching alert to indicate he has found hidden drugs.

TOASTING SUCCESS

"Reward's Rebel Rouser, SchH1, VCCX was the first Boxer, and was the first dog George put a Schutzhund title on. He was only the second Boxer born in America to get a Schutzhund title. He is no longer with us; we lost him at age 11.

"Axel von Bachbett, BH, SchH1, VCCX was the son of Rebel and from our first home-bred litter. He was the first Schutzhund-titled dog for myself and the only Boxer to earn a Schutzhund title in America in 1994. Axel passed away recently, at 11 years of age.

"Grobi vom Hafen, BH, SchH1, FH2, ZTP, AD, O-VCCX is a German import we have had for seven years. (He is nine now.) Grobi's most notable accomplishment is his FH2, the most advanced tracking title a dog can earn in Schutzhund. He was the first Boxer in America to earn it, and among the first dozen of all breeds to do so. He was trained and handled by George.

"Certified Police K9 Ivo vom Hafen, BH, SchH3, IPO3, ZTP, O-VCCX is another dog we imported from Germany as a young adult dog. Ivo has won the USA-BOX Working Boxer Champion of the Year title three years in a row, 1998-2000. His most recent accomplishment was to become certified as a Narcotic Detector Dog. He is trained and handled by George, and is six years old.

GIRL POWER

Xenia von Sparta, BH, SchH3, IPO2, FH1, VCD1, CDX, TD, NA, NAJ, AC, AJC, O-VCCX, certified Police Tracker Dog, is my pride and joy. She came to us from Germany as an 11-week-old puppy, and is now seven years old. I have trained and handled her to all of her titles. She is the first female Boxer in America to make the SchH3 and the IPO. She is the first Boxer of either sex to earn an American Kennel Club (AKC) Versatile Companion Dog (VCD) title, and was the third dog of any breed to do so.

"To earn a VCD, the dog must have separate

Xenia von Sparta BH, SchH3, IPO2, FH1, CDX, TD, NA, NAJ, AC, AJC, O-VCCX holds the 5 lb dumbbell required for the Schutzhund Obedience phase.

Xenia von Sparta retrieves over the scale.

AKC titles in Obedience, Tracking, regular Agility and jumpers with weaves Agility. The American Boxer Club honored her with the 2000 Performance Dog of the Year Award of Merit. She has earned a greater variety of working titles than any other Boxer in history in the U.S. To say I am proud of her is a vast understatement.

POLICE PARTNER

"Certified Police K9 Dolly von den Almeauen, BH, ZTP, AD, O-VCCX was imported by us when she was a little over two years of age. Dolly is the first Boxer that we trained and certified for police work. She is certified in both Narcotic Detection and Tracking, but it is in the area of drug work that she has really made her mark.

"Dolly is six years old and lives with her K9 handler, Investigator Marion Byerson. In the four years she has been at work with the City of LaCrosse Police Department, she has had a 98 percent plus find rate, and has been responsible for taking many, many thousands of dollars worth of illegal drugs off the streets. She is so accurate and reliable, that many other law enforcement departments call her in to work for them as well.

"Dolly has had so many successes in drug detection; she is a local (and among Boxer people, a national) celebrity, and, on her time off, she goes with her handler to anti-drug school programs and helps keep young people from starting drugs. She is an incredible ambassador for the Boxer breed.

HELLO DOLLY

"There are lots of anecdotes about Dolly and her achievements. One day, Dolly and handler Byerson were called out to a traffic stop of a suspected drug dealer. The woman suspect stood outside her car as Byerson approached with Dolly. She was informed that the dog would be searching her vehicle and her person. Her eyes got very wide when they said that, and she immediately admitted to having concealed drugs. As it turned out, she had the drugs hidden in a body cavity, and the thought of Dolly searching her was a bit too disconcerting! Actually, it is surprising how often people give up their drugs without a search when the dog comes on the scene.

"Of course, Dolly and Investigator Byerson have quite a reputation with the local drug people. Recently, when I was searching a state prison camp with Elke, Dolly's daughter, an inmate yelled out, 'Hey, I know that dog! That's Byerson's dog!' As it turns out, Dolly was responsible for the man's incarceration, and he was quite upset to think she was still on his trail!

YOU'RE BUSTED!

"One of Dolly's single largest busts was when she found 65 pounds of a drug called methcathinone or 'KHAT.' A plant material, it comes from Africa, and is chewed. It has an amphetamine-type action that lasts about 24 hours. She uncovered the drug during a search of a shipping company's boxes. This was the first time the drug was discovered in the town, and Dolly had never been trained for detecting this drug!"

Police K9 Dolly von den Almeauen BH, ZTP, AD, O-VCCX and her handler Marion Byerson.

THERAPY DOGS

Therapy dogs are now widely recognized for the important part they play in patient care. Boxers make wonderful therapy dogs. They are sweet and affectionate, and they also have a playful side to their characters. Few people can resist the appeal of the remarkable Boxer face.

CANINE CURE

Sheila Thain is a district nurse who lives on the remote Orkney Islands in Scotland. As well as caring for the sick in her professional life, Sheila also finds the time to visit them socially with her Therapy Dog, Madison, who is a seven-year-old, red and white Boxer.

"I think Boxers have the ideal temperament for therapy work," said Sheila. "They are soft and cuddly, and they are very patient. They like a lot of attention, and respond to everyone."

Sheila has been involved with Boxers for some 40 years, and so she is well versed in the characteristics of the breed.

"I love their enthusiasm," said Sheila. "Boxers never seem to grow up – perhaps that is why they seem to have such a natural affinity with children."

Sheila believes that good, basic training is a must for Boxers.

"If you do not establish control over your Boxer at an early age, you can run into problems," said Sheila. "A Boxer will test the limits, and you must give the necessary guidance so that the dog will mature into a well-behaved adult."

In fact, Sheila has been very successful with her Boxers, training them in Agility and Competitive Obedience, as well as in therapy work. She also runs a dog training class for all breeds.

Sheila is now working with Madison, focusing on Competitive Obedience. But there is still time left for her therapy work.

"I think it is important work to do," said Sheila. "Some patients really look forward to the visits, others are not so bothered. But whatever their reaction, seeing a dog on the ward brings a touch of normality into their lives, which is much needed if you are living in an institution."

Madison: The patients look forward to his visits.

CHAPTER SIX

SEEKING PERFECTION

For the majority of people who own Boxers as companion dogs, the world of breeding and showing seems remote. There are those who enjoy breeding dogs to exhibit in the show ring, but is there any significance beyond winning rosettes? In fact, the answer is a resounding yes!

In the show ring, each breed is judged against its own Breed Standard, which is a written blueprint outlining the physical characteristics and temperament of the "ideal" dog. The winning dog is the one who, in the judge's view, most closely adheres to this ideal.

Of course, no dog is perfect, but the merit of judging against an ideal is to preserve the breed as it was intended to be. It is all too easy for trends to develop, and a certain characteristic to become exaggerated. Or worse still, temperament may become of secondary

importance as breeders strive to produce a "perfect" specimen. The Breed Standard is of vital importance in ensuring that the breed retains its true identity, and its own unique set of characteristics.

The dogs who are successful in the show ring are those who are most likely to be used for breeding. It is their virtues, and their faults, that will be passed on to future generations. It is therefore, plain to see that the future of the breed we love lies in the hands of breeders and exhibitors.

SETTING THE STANDARD

The Boxer Breed Standard varies slightly according to nationality. In the U.K., the Breed Standard is drawn up by the Kennel Club; in the U.S., the American Kennel Club has control. In condensed form, this is what the judge is looking for when he seeks perfection in the show ring.

The Boxer has clean, athletic lines.

on the head, and the shape of the eyes and their expression. It is the Boxer head that puts its unique stamp on the breed.

In outline, the skull should be cleanly covered, and the muzzle should be broad, deep, and powerful. There should be a balance between the muzzle and the skull. The nose is broad, black, and slightly turned up; the cheeks are well developed.

Eyes: Dark brown in color, the eyes should not be too small. The English Standard asks for a "lively, intelligent expression." The American Standard refers to the eyes' "mood-mirroring character" which, when "combined with the wrinkling of the forehead, gives the Boxer head its unique quality of expressiveness."

General Appearance: The Boxer is a smooth-coated, medium-size dog of square build. He has strong bones and well-developed muscles. He gives an impression of great nobility.

Temperament: Alert, dignified and self-assured, the Boxer is playful with his family and friends, but wary with strangers. He has fearless courage if threatened, but is generally an even-tempered, biddable companion.

Head and Face: The Boxer is known as a "head breed," meaning that a great deal of emphasis is placed on the shape of the skull, the formation of the muzzle, the way the ears are set

The cropped ears give the American Boxer a very distinctive look.

The expression should be lively and intelligent.

Forequarters: The shoulders are long and sloping, and the upper arm is long, approaching a right angle to the shoulder blade. The front legs are straight and parallel, with good bone. The elbows should not be too close to the chest.

Body: In profile, the body should be square; the length from the forechest to the rear of the upper thigh should be equal to the height at the wither (the highest point of the body). The back is short, straight, and slightly sloping, and the chest is deep, reaching to the elbows.

Hindquarters: Strong, powerful, and well muscled, the angulation should be in balance with that of the forequarters.

Ears: The ears are set on the highest point of the skull, and set wide apart. In the U.K., they lie flat and close to the cheek, falling forward when the dog is alert. In the U.S., the ears are cropped.

They are cut long and tapering, and give the Boxer a completely different, and dramatic, appearance.

Mouth: The Boxer is one of the few breeds with an undershot jaw, which is a throwback to its Bulldog ancestry. The lower jaw protrudes beyond the upper, and curves slightly upward.

Neck: A strong, muscular neck is required, with an elegant arch that blends smoothly into the withers.

The hindquarters are strong, powerful, and well muscled.

When the Boxer moves, he should reach well forward in front, with a strong drive from the rear.

Feet: Compact and cat-like, with well-arched toes, the feet should turn neither in nor out.

Tail: The tail is set high, and carried forward. It is customarily docked.

Movement: Often referred to as "gait." The Boxer should move with a strong, efficient, ground-covering stride. He should reach well forward in front, with a driving action from the rear.

Color: The Boxer may be fawn or brindle, with white markings which should not exceed one-third of the body. The fawn color may range from light tan or fawn to mahogany. Brindle dogs have black stripes on any of the fawn shades.

Coat: Short and glossy, lying tight to the body.

Size: Males should be 22.5-25 inches (57-63 cm) at the withers; bitches are 21-23.5 inches (53-59 cm). The U.K. Standard limits bitches to 23 inches (59 cm). It also gives a guidelines on weight: males 66-70 pounds (30-32 kg), and bitches 55-60 pounds (25-27 kg).

PLANNING A BREEDING PROGRAM

Now that you know what to aim for, how are you going to set about producing Boxers that conform as closely as possible to the Breed Standard? The sire (father) and dam (mother) will contribute equally to their offspring, so, obviously, both are equally important. Both dog and bitch should be good, typical examples of the breed, with no outstanding faults.

Temperament should be sound on both sides. Pedigrees must be thoroughly investigated to ensure that there are no inherited health conditions that could be passed on to the puppies.

The art of breeding comes down to matching the right dog with the right bitch. The aim is to find dogs that complement each other, cementing the good points, but also seeking to improve on weaker areas. It is vitally important to find out as much as possible about parents, grandparents, and great-grandparents of your breeding stock, as they may exert some influence on the resulting litter.

When breeding pedigree dogs, there are three basic programs to choose from:
• Inbreeding
• Linebreeding
• Outcrossing.

Each program relates to the degree to which the pedigrees of the stud dog and the brood bitch are related. All three options can produce sound, typical dogs, provided that the ancestors in each case are typical of the breed in looks and temperament, and are free from hereditary diseases.

PUPPY TO CHAMPION

After all the hard work of planning a litter, organizing the mating, and then supervising the whelping, hopefully, the breeder has a litter of healthy puppies to rear. Some of the puppies will be sold as pets, others will go to show homes, and the breeder will hope to find a puppy that will do well in the show ring, and will then continue the line. How do you go about finding that puppy? For most breeders, this is a matter of experience. The more litters you breed, the more expert you become at assessing the puppies. Each breeder tends to have his own criteria, and will judge each puppy at around six to eight weeks.

Breeding is a fascinating business, and even the most experienced breeder can get a surprise – good or bad! There is also the "ugly duckling" phase which most Boxer puppies go through, and then it is a matter of keeping your nerve and hoping that your youngster will develop into the beautiful animal you were hoping for.

In the examples on page 99, we have traced a Boxer from his early weeks through to becoming a Champion, to give an idea of how a Boxer develops from puppyhood to maturity.

IN THE SHOW RING

If you are lucky enough to have a top quality Boxer that is worthy of being shown in the ring, you will need to give him special training. You cannot expect an exuberant youngster to work with you amid all the distractions of a show unless you have trained him for the job.

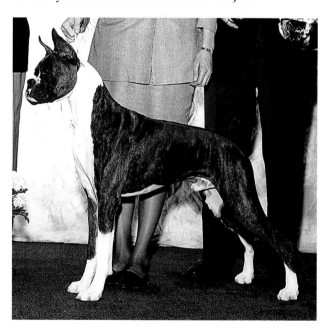

The Boxer must learn to stand in a show pose.

INBREEDING

This is the mating of two very closely related animals, for example, two dogs that have the same sire.

This type of breeding can be used when you want to accentuate – very quickly – a particular trait associated with the family.

Inbreeding should not be attempted by the novice. It requires the skill of experienced breeders who will know detailed histories of the dogs involved, and who will only proceed if they are confident that the resulting offspring will be strong and healthy, as well as being typical specimens of the breed.

Pedigree of Ch. Jenroy Pop My Cork To Walker

Parents	Grandparents	Great-Grandparents	Great-Great-Grandparents
Ch. Tyegarth Glenmorangie Of Jenroy	Ch. Gremlin Summer Storm	Gremlin Famous Footsteps	Ch. Summerdale Shamus
			Gremlin Walk On
		Gremlin Mere Magic	Gremlin Catch Fire
			Gremlin Catch The Dawn
	Tyegarth Old Fashioned	Tyegarth The Tatler	Ch. Gaymitz Jolly Rodger
			Palex Talk Of The Town
		Tyegarth Witches Brew	Tyegarth Brewmaster
			Tyegarth Bitter Brew
Jenroy Whoopsie Daisy	Ch. Tyegarth Glenmorangie Of Jenroy	Ch. Gremlin Summer Storm	Gremlin Famous Footsteps
			Gremlin Mere Magic
		Tyegarth Old Fashioned	Tyegarth The Tatler
			Tyegarth Witches Brew
	Jenroy Bumps A 'Daisy	Ch. Gremlin Summer Storm	Gremlin Famous Footsteps
			Gremlin Mere Magic
		Dunsacre Andromeda Of Jenroy	Tyegarth Cornbrew
			Swanson Blue Jade

OUTCROSSING

This is the mating of totally unrelated dogs. As you can see from the pedigree below, these parents of Ch. Glenfall the Gladiator have no relatives in common.

It is a method of introducing completely new blood to a line and if you produce the result you are hoping for, you can fix the type by linebreeding.

Ch. Glenfall The Gladiator: the result of out-crossing.

Parents	Grandparents	Great-Grandparents	Great-Great-Grandparents
Ch. Kinbra Uncle Sam Of Winuwuk	Kreyons Back In Town Of Winuwuk	Int. Ch. Scher-khouns Shadrack	Int. Ch. Millans Fashion Hint
			Int. Ch. Scher-khouns Carousel
		U.S. Ch. Kreyons Firebrand	U.S. Ch. Cajons Calling Card
			Bartizans Jewel
	Kinbra Alice Blue Gown	Kitwe Blue Mink	Int. Ch. Seefeld Picasso
			Wilrait Copper Velvet
		Kinbra Alice Springs	Gremlin Jolly Swagman
			Kinbra Drury Lane
Glenfall Amber Spirit	Ch. Tyegarth Famous Grouse	Ch. Gremlin Summer Storm	Gremlin Famous Footsteps
			Gremlin Mere Magic
		Tyegarth Old Fashioned	Tyegarth The Tatler
			Tyegarth Witches Brew
	Tyegarth Hundred Pipers	Steynmere Midnight Major	Ch. Tyegarth Famous Grouse
			Steynmere Moonfire
		Tyegarth Prohibition	Tyegarth Cossack
			Tyegarth Leading Article

LINEBREEDING

This is similar to inbreeding in that it involves members of the same family, but they are not so closely related. This is the most commonly used breeding program as it retains the virtues of the line, but also introduces new blood.

Bucksteps Broderie Anglaise: An example of line-breeding.

Parents	Grandparents	Great-Grandparents	Great-Great-Grandparents
Bucksteps Top Hat	Bucksteps Going For Gold At Glenfall	Ch. Glenfall The Gladiator	Ch. Kinbra Uncle Sam Of Winuwuk
			Glenfall Amber Spirit
		Bucksteps No No Nanette	Ch. Tyegarth Famous Grouse
			Bucksteps Miss Brodie
	Bucksteps Hot Gossip	Ch. Carinya Rye 'n Dry	Ch. Tyegarth Glenmorangie Of Jenroy
			Change Key Of Gremlin
		Bucksteps Easy Virtue	Ch. Glenfall The Gladiator
			Bucksteps No No Nanette
Bucksteps Black Bess	Bucksteps Going For Gold At Glenfall	Ch. Glenfall The Gladiator	Ch. Kinbra Uncle Sam Of Winuwuk
			Glenfall Amber Spirit
		Bucksteps No No Nanette	Ch. Tyegarth Famous Grouse
			Bucksteps Miss Brodie
	Bucksteps Bubble Gum	Ch. Bucksteps Charlie Brown	Ch. Carinya Rye 'n' Dry
			Bucksteps Easy Virtue
		Bucksteps Quality Street	Bucksteps Going For Gold At Glenfall
			Bucksteps Starkers

PUPPY TO CHAMPION
Ch. Norwatch Sunhawk Showtime

◀ Eight weeks: A promising pup, the brindling is still quite indistinct.

Eleven months: Beautifully constructed, but ▶ still lacking substance. He won the East of England Championship Show, beating an overall entry of 397 puppies.

◀ Two and a half years: Won his first Challenge Certificate at 19 months and became a Champion when this photo was taken. He has now won six CCs and one Reserve CC.

THE AMERICAN DREAM

Paula Rossman, who is based in Illinois, is relatively new to Boxers, but her Cinema kennel has already enjoyed considerable success, and she is working hard at planning a breeding program that will produce top quality dogs that are sound in both mind and body.

"We have been in Boxers since 1995; we owned Irish Wolfhounds prior to that," said Paula. "We started showing in 1996, and had our first litter in 1997. Our elderly neighbors had Boxers when I was a child, and I always wanted one of those proud-looking dogs, who seemed so regal, yet playful. I was about eight or so when I announced I wanted one to my mother, who promptly responded, as so many moms respond to similar announcements, with, 'When you get your own place, you can own whatever you want!'

"The most important dog in our kennel is Nell, registered as Firestar's Raisin' Nell. Nell, our foundation bitch, was bought from Diane Boyle of Firestar Boxers in 1995. Nell has produced two

Champions to date, with four more of her pups continuing to show as of this year. She started it all, with her first win (Grand Sweepstakes at a Boxer Specialty!).

"Our most important and only male is Cosmo – HiMaster's Fired Up at Cinema. He was purchased from California, and showed totally in the Illinois area. Along the way, he won two Best Puppy in Sweeps, an uncountable amount of RWDs, three majors, and he just needs his three singles.

"The main reason we consider him successful is that he has been shown a minimum of times, and has had a good number of wins. More importantly, Cosmo is my 'special' Boxer because of his temperament, attitude, showiness, and the fact that he is the most wonderful dog to live with!

"Cosmo is also going to be a huge influence on our breeding program. We have a litter planned for this year that has been 'in the making' since 1999, when we bred Nell back to Cosmo's

Cosmo: Hi Master's Fired Up At Cinema.

grandsire (in anticipation of breeding a pup from Nell back to him). Our whole kennel is based on the solid foundation of these two dogs, but more so on the lines behind them."

Paula spends a lot of time planning for the future, although she is realistic about how quickly progress can be made. "Our goals are to simply improve the breed, and to have each generation be a little better than the one before," she said. "Often, I plan litters with the understanding that I am not going to end up with all the improvements I am trying to make in one generation, or in one litter, but rather, we view each litter as a 'step' closer to what our vision of the ideal Boxer is.

"We have learned to keep our minds on our own breeding programs, and to avoid much of the 'goings-on' and trends. We keep our minds set on our ideal, and we keep our eyes open to watch for dogs that will help us achieve the results we desire. We have been lucky to have had access to the studs we have used to date, and to have had such wonderful results in the few litters we have bred."

Every successful breeder needs a good eye for a show puppy, but in the breeding game there are no certainties. "I like to watch puppies grow up, and watch them at different stages, but usually I try and make a decision around 8-10 weeks of age," said Paula. "Of course, the best way to get a show dog is to buy an adult, but with puppies you must concentrate on trying to assess potential – that is all you can go on. Too many people try to 'guarantee' a winner at the age of eight weeks, but it can't be done.

"I look for a puppy who is 'together' at eight weeks, and is well balanced, with adequate front and rear angles. I was told that, when evaluating young Boxer heads, and looking down on to the Boxer head, it should resemble a 'bunny' with the ears pulled back! There are many 'little' things we look for, and it varies from one breeder to the next. I always look at toplines, tail sets, and short backs, because these are priorities in my breeding program. Another breeder may have different priorities, and therefore seek different strong points in a pup."

A Boxer may be a wonderful specimen of the breed, but he must be able to show himself to advantage in the ring. Paula picked up the following tip from a Great Dane breeder, who runs a handling class. "It involves teaching your dog to 'free-stack,' by saying, . . . 'Ready . . . Set. . . GO! I train all my dogs this way, and they all free-stack amazingly well."

You can learn a great deal about a breed by watching dogs in the ring, but it is important not to fall into the trap of 'fault-judging.' "I was taught to look for the dog with the most merits in the ring," said Paula. "You must never sit ringside and fault-judge, which means you sit and pick out every fault on every dog in the ring . . . it's a bad habit to start. Instead, I was taught to look for the positive qualities each dog in the ring possesses, and to place them according to that.

Merlot Cinema's Ecco Domani: A young prospect at the Cinema kennel.

Show Pose

To begin with, your Boxer must learn to stand in show pose. This is a position where the Boxer stands in profile with his legs in line with each other, and his head looking slightly upward, focusing on the handler. The reason for the show pose is that it gives the judge the best picture of a dog's general outline and conformation.

In the U.K. and the U.S., dogs are "stacked." This means they are physically placed in the correct position, and the handler keeps them in the show pose by using a short lead and holding up the tail. A Boxer must be happy with this procedure in order to show himself off to advantage, so the best plan is to start training while the puppy is still young.

Puppy Training

Most puppies from show homes are used to being placed in an informal pose from an early age. This is done so the breeder can assess each puppy and work out which is most likely to succeed in the show ring. When you start training your Boxer, make sure you are armed with some tasty treats. It is important to find something your puppy really loves – cheese or liver, for example – and use it only when you are show training, or when you are in the ring. In this way, your Boxer will be really keen to get the treat, and will try his hardest.

Use the treat to encourage the puppy to stand, and, as you give the reward, the pup will maintain his position. As soon as you are happy with his pose, give the command "Stand." Always keep training sessions short, and finish

The first step is for the puppy to be placed in an informal show pose.

with a game. The last thing you want is a dog who appears bored or switched off when you ask him to go into show pose.

In Europe, dogs are shown "free-standing." This means they are walked into position, and they maintain their position on a loose lead. Obviously, this takes a lot of hard work to achieve, but it does look very effective in the ring.

Hands-on

The judge will line up all the dogs in a class and look at them in show pose. He will then examine each dog individually. This involves a thorough "hands-on" examination so the judge can evaluate each dog in detail. He will open the mouth to look at the teeth, examine the eyes and ears, and then feel the Boxer's body, assessing shoulder placement, depth of chest, topline, breadth of ribs, tail set, and

The judge will take a careful look at movement, as this can also reveal a lot about the way a dog is put together.

hindquarters. In male dogs, he will check to see if the testicles are descended.

The show Boxer must submit to being examined by a total stranger without becoming tense or unsettled. This is a lot to ask, so it is helpful if show puppies are routinely examined, first by members of the family, and then by friends, so they get used to being handled. It is a good idea to join a ring training class so that your puppy can get used to being examined by strangers.

On the Move

After the individual examination, the judge will want to see each Boxer move. The way a dog moves reveals a lot about conformation, as well as showing if the dog has the correct Boxer gait. Generally, a judge will want to see the dog's movement in profile, coming toward him, and moving away from him. For this reason, the handler is often asked to gait the dog in a triangle.

The Boxer must show an efficient, ground-covering stride, with his front legs reaching out, his hindquarters driving from behind, and his feet keeping close to the ground. Practice with your Boxer in the yard and at ring-training classes so that you move in unison, keeping pace with your dog rather than dragging him from behind, or rushing to keep up with him. Try to keep your Boxer on a loose lead so that he moves freely and without interference.

Preparing for a Show

The Boxer is a wonderfully low-maintenance breed, and there is little to do to get him ready for a show. You want your dog to be clean and sweet-smelling, so give him a bath in the run-up to a show. Make sure you bathe a couple of days before the show, as the coat will need a chance to settle down and regain its natural oils.

On the day before the show, use a stripping comb along the line of the dog's neck and down his back legs. This gets rid of any loose hairs and helps to give a clean-cut outline. Then take a grooming glove and work briskly all over the body. You can follow this up by using a piece of velvet or chamois leather and rubbing it over the coat to bring up the shine.

Most Boxers benefit from a general trimming,

Clippers are used to give the Boxer's face a smooth, clean outline.

which can be done using dog clippers. Take the clipppers over the muzzle to remove whiskers and eyebrows. Then use them behind the elbows, and along the line of the undercarriage. Use a pair of scissors to trim the feathers from the back of the legs, and to tidy up the tail.

In the U.S., trimming has become something of an art form, while, in the U.K., a more basic procedure is followed. Regardless of your method, the result should be a sleek, glossy Boxer, showing a smart, clean-cut outline.

Making a Champion

Every breeder and exhibitor's dream is to have their dog made up into a Champion. In the U.K., this means winning three Challenge Certificates (CCs) under three separate judges. In the U.S., a dog must win a total of 15 points, which must include two "majors" (3, 4, or 5 point wins) under different judges. The number of points available depends on the breed and the location of the show.

Sportsmanship

At the highest level, showing is very competitive, and, although there is no prize money involved, feelings can run high. Make sure you and your dog enjoy going to shows rather than becoming stressed out by winning or losing. A show is a great opportunity to meet other Boxer enthusiasts, and you will also learn a lot by watching other Boxers in the ring.

The judge will evaluate each dog by assessing how closely it conforms to the Breed Standard, but, obviously, he is working on his own interpretation of the Standard. There will, doubtless, be a type of Boxer he prefers, and even though you have a top quality animal, you may not win on the day. This is part of the fascination of showing – after all, it would be very dull if the same Boxer won all the time!

If you are lucky enough to win or to be placed, enjoy your triumph. If it is not your day, make sure you are the first to congratulate the winners, and remember, win or lose, you are taking the same dog home with you – and there are always lots more shows to have a go at!

Claire Kay has been involved with Boxers all her life. Her mother, Audrey Stephenson, founded the Seacrest kennel in 1962, and Claire took over the kennel name in 1983. It was always a well-respected kennel, but in the last ten years it has gone from strength to strength and Claire has won three top breeder awards in the last two years.

"I was bought up in a house full of Boxers so I didn't choose the breed, it chose me," said Claire. In fact, horses were the first love of her life, and although she loved Boxers as pets, she was not initially interested in showing them. "I got dragged to shows as a toddler, but, as soon as I was old enough to be left at home, I preferred to be with the horses," she said.

The family moved to the Yorkshire Dales, and Claire started working in a racing stable. This is where she met her husband, John, and it seemed that her future lay in the horse world. All that changed when a riding accident left her with permanent back injuries. She could not return to her job, and was left at home with a lot of time on her hands.

"We had been given a Boxer puppy as a wedding present, and, because I had nothing else to do, I started training her and was encouraged to take her to shows," said Claire. "We were pretty successful in the ring at Open Show level, and we even won three firsts at three Championship shows. The bitch was not of top quality and did not have the bloodlines that I liked, but I was well and truly bitten by the showing bug.

"My mother would not allow me to take over the Seacrest kennel name without proving my commitment and ability, so I had to serve an 'apprenticeship' of sorts. For a year, I concentrated on improving my handling and learning more about the breed. When the year was up, I went to a show with my mother, and I had to point out all the dogs I liked, and give reasons for why I liked them. The result of this exercise was me taking over the Seacrest prefix, and also determining which bloodlines I wanted to use in my own breeding program."

The first Champion in the kennel was Ch. Comedy Of Errors From Skelder, a bitch bought from the well-known breeder Joy Malcolm. She went on to win five Challenge Certificates, including the bitch CC at Crufts in 1991. Claire's second Champion, Ch. Tyegarth Pacherenc At Seacrest, came from Sheila Cartwright's top-producing kennel, and gained his title in six weeks. He went on to become top sire in the breed from 1994 to 1997, gaining seven national awards in that four-year period, and stamping his distinctive mark on many different bloodlines.

Claire showed his most successful son, Ch. Huttonvale High Command At Seacrest, and he won an amazing 18 Challenge Certificates. He was Top Dog in 1994, and Dog of the Year in 1995 and 1996.

The bloodlines have been strengthened over the years by the inclusion of a number of CC and Reserve CC winning Boxers who have made their mark in the ring as well as being excellent producers. Other Champions who have contributed to the kennel's success are: Ch. Seacrest Sassafras At Quantro, Ch. Seacrest Double Trigger From Glenfall, Ch. Seacrest In The Wings At Alcomar, and Ch. Seacrest Danoli At Carmondene, who won nine CCs, including Best of Breed and Group 3 at Crufts in 1999.

The Seacrest set-up is not representative of most successful show kennels. Claire does not like her dogs to live outside in kennels, and yet she has far too many for them all to live in the house. She has therefore developed a system where the stud dogs, the current show team, and the puppies all live at her home, and the brood bitches live locally with friends and family. "That way, every one has a place by the fire," said Claire. "My dogs are first and

Ch. Huttonvale High Command At Seacrest: Winner of 18 CCs, 18 Reserve CCs, Top Dog 94, Runner-up 95, 96, Dog of the Year 95, 96.

foremost pets, who just happen to be very good at showing," she said. "I don't impose too many rules – you don't visit my house unless you want to wear a Boxer. I like to keep their natural exuberance for life to the fore. My dogs always show their socks off because they enjoy what they are doing."

The best dog Claire has shown is Ch. Huttonvale High Command At Seacrest, who gained his first CC when he was only ten months old. "Everybody loved Daz," said Claire. "He was such a clown in the ring and loved showing off." The most influential dog in the kennel was undoubtedly his sire, Ch. Tyegarth Pacherenc At Seacreast. "Pash was more famous for his success as a producer," said Claire. "He could consistently pass on his virtues, without necessarily passing on his faults. He also had the ideal Boxer temperament. He had great courage and dignity, and he was always happy, calm, and never aggressive – a real gentleman."

Claire does not begin seriously evaluating her prospective show puppies until they are seven weeks of age. "I like to get the pets in the litter placed with their new families at seven weeks, then I can concentrate on the favored few," she said. Claire sets the pups up in show pose and then weighs up their faults and their virtues. "At this stage, I am looking for correct proportions, with the torso standing over the limbs, not on top of them. Many dogs have good points, rarely do they flow into each other, giving overall balance that will be so important in the show ring."

Claire spends a lot of time with the puppies between seven and nine weeks. "I think this is the best time to look at a Boxer puppy as they can change so much between nine weeks and nine months, particularly the unique Boxer head," she said. "However, by the time they have passed nine months, they have regained their correct proportions.

"Obviously, this is not an exact science, and there is always a fair amount of trial and error involved. If I like a puppy at nine weeks, I will run it on for a few months to see how it develops. If it still looks promising, that's great; if not, I will find it a suitable pet home. Of course, you want to produce winners, but the most important thing is for the dogs to be loved and appreciated as family companions."

CHAPTER SEVEN

HEALTH CARE

By Trevor Turner
Bvet Med MRCVS

I t should never be forgotten that the Boxer, an exuberant extrovert, full of fun and overflowing with energy, is essentially a working dog. The Boxer was bred originally in Germany as a guard, basically unknown in both Britain and the U.S. until after the Second World War. Once introduced, the breed soon shot to popularity on both sides of the Atlantic; a popularity which has been maintained ever since. In 1999, 35,000 were registered in America and nearly 10,000 in Britain, making the Boxer the most popular dog in the Working Group in the U.K.

Not surprisingly, in such a numerically large breed, breed-specific problems do occur, which will be dealt with later in the chapter.

PREVENTATIVE CARE

Preventative care, to any owner of a new Boxer puppy, usually means vaccination and "deworming." In fact it involves much more than this. Breed Standards on both sides of the

Atlantic make reference to the lively, strong, well-muscled appearance with powerful movement. In other words, this dog needs – and must have – adequate exercise. This should be considered as part of preventative health care, together with an adequate and, above all, a well-balanced diet in order that the adult Boxer does not become overweight. This in itself can exacerbate any potential heart or joint problems.

Exercise

The Boxer is not for those of "couch potato" mentality. Adaptable by nature and eager to please, you would find that your dog would soon adopt the same habits. Obesity and its attendant problems will then undoubtedly follow. On the other hand, no growing puppies should be overexercised, as it can cause damage to their joints.

Therefore, although these exuberant extroverts are eager to join in any boisterous children's

games, caution should be exercised with your Boxer puppy and advice from the breeder and/or your veterinarian strictly followed. Once their bones have ceased growing, then exercise levels have to be increased to maintain condition.

Diet

Diet is also important. Follow the breeder's advice initially. At the time of primary vaccinations, discuss diet and carefully follow any advice given by your vet. Because of that "adaptable nature and extrovert, outgoing personality," it is very easy to overdo the treats at the expense of a proper balanced diet. Coupled with underexercise, the result is the not uncommon fat Boxer straining heart, limbs, and lungs alike. Prevention in this instance is far better than cure.

Vaccination

Dogs, like people, develop a natural immunity as the result of exposure to disease. For example, infectious tracheobronchitis, (kennel cough) is extremely contagious, but seldom life-threatening in the otherwise healthy dog. However, it does cause a nasty, persistent, contagious cough that can be troublesome in the Boxer, a brachycephalic (flat-faced) breed. Coughing in the breed is to be avoided wherever possible, if only because Boxers can be prone to certain types of heart condition which coughing can exacerbate.

In the healthy dog, recovery and a strong immunity will develop as a result of natural infection and that will last for about six months.

The flat-faced Boxer may be more troubled by coughing than other breeds.

The same principle applies with other diseases. Distemper is a considerably more serious disease than kennel cough and, before vaccination was routine, it was common in the dog population. Following natural infection, a number of dogs inevitably died. Those that survived had a solid immunity, which was continuously reinforced by contact with other dogs carrying the virus which was so prevalent. Years ago, distemper was not the only common canine killer disease, but, with the introduction of ever more efficacious vaccination, many of these diseases are now, thankfully, things of the past.

Vaccination (inoculation) stimulates the dog to produce active immunity against one or, as is more common today, a collection of diseases without developing any signs of disease.

Natural immunity is acquired from the dam and is boosted by suckling.

The puppy acquires some immunity from the dam while in the womb. After birth, immunity is topped up (boosted) all the time the puppy suckles. This is passive immunity. Once weaning takes place, this soon fades and that is when the puppy should receive primary vaccination to stimulate his own immunity. This will protect him just as natural immunity protected the dog that survived actual disease.

This immunity does not last forever. Largely as the result of vaccination, many serious canine killer diseases are no longer rife and therefore natural challenge does not occur. Regular boosters are thus essential to ensure immunity.

Inoculation

Strictly, inoculation means introducing an agent into the tissues of the body to stimulate an immune response. This usually involves an injection, but human smallpox vaccine, for example, was introduced by scarifying the skin of the arm and not by injection.

Vaccination similarly stimulates the subject to produce immunity against a disease without developing signs, but need not necessarily be directly introduced into the tissues of the body. Thus, returning to kennel cough as an example, vaccination is achieved by instilling a few drops up the nose.

Primary vaccination

Primary vaccination should be started as soon as the passively acquired immunity from the mother has declined sufficiently to allow the puppy to develop his own active immunity. If vaccinated too early, circulating maternal antibodies destroy the vaccine and no protection develops. Then, when passive immunity subsequently wanes, the puppy is totally unprotected.

Vaccination takes time to stimulate active immunity, and it is during this period that the puppy is vulnerable to infection. This immunity gap occurs at the same time that the puppy should be introduced to as many new experiences as possible, to ensure that he matures into a well-integrated family dog. Boxers are a working breed with natural guarding instincts, and, in order that he accepts strangers with as much equanimity as the family, early socialization is essential. Vaccines that will stimulate active immunity in the puppy, even in the face of circulating maternal antibodies, are now available. The course can be started as early as six weeks and the pup will be fully protected by ten weeks of age.

The timing of vaccination depends on disease prevalence in the area.

The timing of vaccination and the vaccine used depends on disease prevalence in the area, together with other disease factors, as well as the puppy. Call your local vet and ask about vaccination policy. You can also discuss appointment details, prices, and facilities. Ask if the practice organizes puppy classes or knows where these are available. These are socialization classes where your bouncy Boxer puppy will learn at least a few fundamentals of canine etiquette.

Booster vaccinations

Vaccination shots do not last forever. It is for this reason that vets advise reinoculation (boosters). The problem is, when and how frequently?

Traditionally, vets have recommended routine, annual, across-the-board boosting. Recently, boosters have become a matter of concern both for veterinarians and dog owners alike. Polyvalent (multivalent) vaccines give protection against a collection of diseases. They are very popular and economical, costing considerably less (in terms of cash, time, and stress) than separate injections against each of the inoculable diseases. However, recently both their necessity and safety have been questioned.

Vets are recommended to follow manufacturers' instructions with any drug, including vaccines. In order to obtain a product license, so that the vaccine may be marketed, manufacturers have to submit evidence regarding safety and efficacy for the product. With a vaccine, this includes duration of immunity. The latter, due to cost and other factors, is usually examined over twelve months; hence, when a product license is issued, recommendations will advise boosting after one year.

This procedure is presently under review by manufacturers. Some are suggesting that, with certain diseases (e.g., distemper and hepatitis), annual boosters may not be strictly necessary. Professionally, and this view is based on more than forty years of busy canine practice, I have to say that the risk of reaction is so slight

If you are concerned about booster inoculations, discuss the matter with your vet.

compared with the threat of disease in unprotected dogs, that I would rather go for over-vaccination than have to relive my personal experiences of major canine epidemics.

However, if you have concerns, discuss them with your vet at the time of primary vaccination. Your views will be respected and the risks and benefits with respect to your particular pet, according to disease prevalence in your area, will be examined.

As a result of the investigations into reactions following vaccination, information is beginning to emerge that certain breeds appear to be more reaction-prone than others. I am happy to say that the Boxer is not among these.

Measuring immunity

The need for vaccination/revaccination (boosting) can be accurately determined with blood tests. However, be forewarned. It is likely that the cost of testing for each of the diseases will be as much as a combined booster against all of them. Money apart, it is also arguable whether blood tests are in the dog's best interests. Although less than a teaspoonful of blood is required for several tests, taking the sample is considerably more stressful for your dog than one quick and simple booster injection under the skin.

Core and non-core vaccines – greater and lesser essentials

The veterinary profession today acknowledges that there are drawbacks associated with some vaccines. In consequence, there has been a move to divide vaccination into two groups, essential vaccines (core vaccines) and less essential (non-core) vaccines. Core (essential) vaccines are those that protect against diseases that are serious, fatal, or difficult to treat.

In Britain, these include distemper, parvovirus, and adenovirus (hepatitis). In the U.S., rabies is also included in this category. With the change in quarantine laws in the U.K., rabies vaccine may well become a core vaccine in the not too distant future.

Non-core vaccines include bordetella, leptospirosis, coronavirus, and borrelia (Lyme disease). This latter vaccine is used widely in North America and is known to cause reactions in a number of dogs. Lyme disease is caused by bacteria which are transmitted through the bites of certain ticks. Relatively rare in Britain, it is very common in certain parts of the U.S.

Contagious diseases

Bordetella (Kennel Cough)

Also known as infectious tracheobronchitis, this is not usually life-threatening except in very young and elderly dogs. The signs are usually a persistent cough lasting about three weeks. In the U.K., bordetella bronchiseptica, a bacterial organism, is considered the primary cause with viruses implicated as secondaries. In the U.S., parainfluenza virus is considered the main cause with bordetella as a secondary invader.

Today, both in the U.K. and the U.S., most multivalent vaccines include a parainfluenza component. The bordetella vaccine is administered separately via nasal drops, which have been shown to give a better immunity than conventional vaccination by injection. Recently introduced on both sides of the Atlantic is a combined parainfluenza and bordetella vaccine, again in the form of nasal drops.

Canine Distemper

In developed countries such as the U.S. and Britain, canine distemper is no longer as widespread as previously. This is entirely due to preventative vaccination. Signs (symptoms) vary. Fever, diarrhea, coughing, discharges from the nose and eyes are all seen. Sometimes the pads of the feet will harden, a sign of the so-called hardpad variant. Fits, chorea (twitching of groups of muscles) and paralysis can be seen in a high proportion of infected dogs. The virus can also be implicated in the so-called kennel cough syndrome.

Kennel cough is highly infectious and spreads rapidly from dog to dog.

Hepatitis

Canine Hepatitis, better known in America as adenovirus disease, can show signs ranging from sudden death with peracute infection to mild cases where the patient is just a bit "off-color." Most cases present with fever, enlargement of all the lymph glands, and a swollen liver. During recovery, the clear part of the eye (cornea) can become oedematous (fluid-filled) and appear cloudy. Thus, the dog may look blind. This "blue eye" is very worrisome for any owner, but usually resolves quickly without impairing sight. Adenovirus can also be a component of the kennel cough syndrome.

Canine parvovirus (CPV)

A relatively new disease, it was first recognized in 1978, and in the 1980s caused problems worldwide. It is caused by a virus that can exist in the environment for a considerable time. Signs include vomiting and diarrhea, often with blood (dysentery). Control of this disease is largely one of the unsung triumphs of modern veterinary medicine, for it has been undoubtedly due to the rapid development of highly effective vaccines.

Rabies

Rabies is present on all continents except Australia and Antarctica. Several countries, of which the U.K. is one, are free of the disease. The virus does not survive long outside the body. The disease is transmitted by wildlife, e.g., foxes, or in some parts of the world, stray dogs. Transmission is mainly by biting. This is

In the U.S., it is mandatory to vaccinate your dog against rabies.

an extremely serious disease communicable to humans (zoonotic), which disrupts the central nervous system. Vaccination, using an inactivated (killed) vaccine, is mandatory in many countries including the United States. In Britain, it has not yet become mandatory to have your dog vaccinated against rabies unless you wish to travel to certain authorized countries and return to Britain under the PETS Travel Scheme.

Lyme Disease

This is a tick-borne bacterial disease. It causes acute, often recurrent, polyarthritis in both dogs and humans. Fever, cardiac, kidney, and neurological problems can occur in some cases. A vaccine is available in the U.S.

Coronavirus disease

Coronaviral gastroenteritis occurs worldwide, but the signs are milder than those of parvovirus. It usually affects younger dogs, 6 to 12 weeks old, and in some kennels 100 percent of the dogs may be affected. Spontaneous recovery occurs in 7 to 10 days although diarrhea may persist for several weeks. There is no licensed vaccine available in the U.K., although vaccines are available in America.

PARASITES

Routine parasite control is an important part of preventative care for any dog. Ectoparasites, e.g., lice, fleas and ticks, are not quite such a problem in the Boxer as in some of the more full-coated breeds, e.g., Collies and Sheepdogs.

Nevertheless, ectoparasite control should not be neglected in your Boxer. Parasite control also includes treatment for endoparasites. These include roundworms, tapeworms and hookworms, together with heartworm, which is important in Southern Europe and North America.

ECTOPARASITES

Fleas

Fleas are the most common ectoparasite found on dogs. Some dogs can carry very high flea burdens without showing any signs, whereas others will develop flea allergy dermatitis (FAD) from only one or two flea bites. FAD is

Puppy and adult Boxers will need routine treatment to control parasites.

primarily an allergic response, and Boxers do have a reputation for suffering from certain allergic conditions, so flea control should not be ignored.

Fleas are not host specific. Both dog and cat fleas can be found on dogs, cats, and humans. They can be picked up from urban gardens (yards) since hedgehogs, squirrels, and racoons can all act as vectors. If in need of a blood meal, which is essential for the completion of its life cycle, the opportunist flea is just as likely to hop on to us as our pets. To be effective, flea control must involve both the adult fleas on the

The dog flea – Ctenocephalides canis.

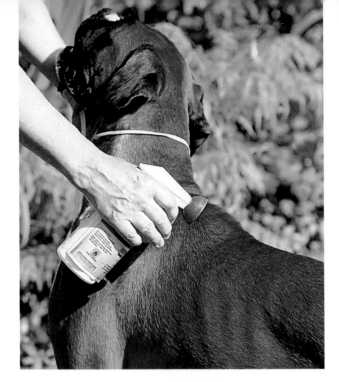

Fleas can be treated with a spray.

Spot-on preparations are becoming more popular.

dog and also the immature stages, which develop in the home environment. Having dined on the blood of the host, the female flea then commences egg laying. This may be on the dog, or, as is more likely, she will hop off to lay eggs in the environment. If laid on your Boxer, due to the short coat, the eggs will soon drop off to develop in the carpets and crevices of your home.

Development can be as short as three weeks, depending on temperature and humidity. Once developed in suitable environments, fleas can survive for more than a year without feeding. This is the reason why pets, and people, are sometimes bitten when entering empty properties previously occupied by pets.

Flea control

Control in the home should include thorough vacuuming to remove immature stages. The use

of an insecticide with prolonged action to kill any developing fleas is worthwhile. Few insecticides presently on the market kill flea larvae. Your dog must also be treated, and this can take several forms.

• Oral medications, which prevent completion of the life cycle of the flea.
• Applications in the form of sprays, spot-on liquids or powders.
• Insecticidal baths.

Bathing has little residual effect and therefore should be combined with some other method of flea control. Spot-on preparations are very popular. They use sophisticated technology to disperse the chemical over an invisible fat layer which covers the skin. The chemical does not actually enter the body. Within 24 hours of application, the dog will have total protection against fleas for approximately two months, and this protection will survive two or three routine baths. When a flea bites the dog, its mouth parts have to penetrate through the fat layer to get to the blood and thus, it ingests the chemical.

Many effective flea preparations are available over-the-counter from pet stores and supermarkets, but it is still worthwhile discussing strategy with your vet. Many of the longer lasting, more effective compounds are available from veterinarians only. Your vet will also be much more aware of the flea problem in the locality and will be able to work out a control strategy with you.

Lice

Lice are not as common as fleas. They are uncommon in Boxers, except poorly reared puppies. They do not survive away from the host and therefore require direct contact for transmission. The eggs (nits) are attached to individual hairs. Infestation causes intense itching. Examination of the hair, particularly around the ears, head, and over the shoulders, usually reveals the lice or the nits stuck to the base of the hairs. Ectoparasiticidal shampoos are effective, but do not forget to wash bedding and spray with an appropriate product.

Ticks

These can be a problem in some areas, both in the U.K. and North America. They are important since they can be the carriers of various diseases such as Lyme disease (particularly common in the U.S.), babesiosis and ehrlichiosis. The two latter diseases are now significant in Britain due to the freedom of

Dogs that live in rural areas are more likely to become infested with harvest mites.

travel for pets to certain parts of Europe and other authorized countries under the PETS Travel Scheme. Some flea and louse preparations are also licensed for tick control, and there are spot-on preparations available which have prolonged activity even if you bathe your dog between applications.

Harvest Mites

Boxers are prone to harvest mite infestation, particularly if they are exercised in fields and woodland locations with chalky subsoil in the autumn (fall). The feet and the muzzle are most frequently affected. The parasite is the immature form (larva) of a mite that freely lives in decaying organic matter. The tiny, red larvae are just visible to the naked eye and cause intense irritation. Continuous licking of the feet or rubbing of the muzzle can result in secondary infection and sometimes sores that are quite difficult to clear up. Prolonged action insecticidal sprays are effective.

Mange

This is a parasitic skin disease caused by mites. The two types that most commonly occur in dogs are demodectic mange and sarcoptic mange.

The demodectic mite lives in the hair follicles and generally causes no harm. However, when the animal's immune system is compromised, the mites can cause hair loss, particularly around the face and eyes. Fortunately, this type of mange is not especially itchy or contagious. There are very effective remedies, but treatment must be under veterinary supervision.

Sarcoptic mange causes intense itching and is highly contagious to humans. Spread by direct contact, the main source of infection is wildlife, such as foxes. Treatment involves repeated antiparasitic dips or shampoos, which your vet will prescribe.

Cheyletiellosis or "walking dandruff"

This is not an uncommon condition in Boxer puppies. The surface-living mite can just be seen with the naked eye. Look along the back and underparts; there is always excess dandruff in which the mites will be found. Treatment with any of the ectoparasiticidal preparations results

All puppies need to be treated for roundworm.

in rapid cure. The condition is important because it is a zoonosis, i.e., it affects humans, particularly children, who are often affected on the abdomen as a result of cuddling their newly acquired Boxer puppy.

ENDOPARASITES

Roundworms

Dogs and worms are virtually synonymous in many people's minds – and certain roundworms are ubiquitous in puppies. There are several types, but the most common is *Toxocara canis*, which is a large, round, white worm 3–6 inches (7 to 15 cm) long. The life cycle is complex and includes migration through the tissues of the host. Larvae (immature worms) can remain dormant in the tissues for long periods. In the pregnant bitch, under hormonal influence, these dormant larvae become activated and cross the placenta into the unborn puppy. There they develop into adult worms in the small intestine. Thus, puppies who are only ten days old can shed infected roundworm eggs. Larvae are also passed from the bitch to the puppy via the milk during suckling.

Vets advise regular worming of litters from approximately two weeks of age. Treatment should be repeated regularly until the puppy is at least six months old. Because of a slight risk of infection in man, adult dogs should be routinely wormed about twice a year. Adult dogs become reinfected from sniffing infected faeces, but show few signs. Puppies may show signs of malnutrition if heavily infected, despite the fact that they are eating well. A distended abdomen ("pot belly"), diarrhea, vomiting, obstruction of the bowel, and even death, can occur.

Effective preparations are available without prescription, but it is still worthwhile discussing control with your vet, who will supply prescription preparations that cover roundworms, and a whole variety of other worms, with a single dose.

Tapeworms (Cestodes)

These are the other important class of worms

Your vet will give advice about all worming treatments and the precautions you should take.

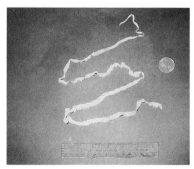

Tapeworm passed by an adult dog. (The coin gives an indication of size.)

found in the dog. Unlike roundworms, they have an indirect life cycle, i.e., they cannot be spread from dog to dog directly, but require intermediate hosts. These range from fleas, sheep, horses, rodents, and sometimes even humans, depending on the type of tapeworm involved.

The most common tapeworm of the dog (and cat), *Dipylidium caninum*, uses the flea as the intermediate host. The mature worm lives in the intestine and can measure up to 20 inches (50 cm). Eggs are contained within mature segments, which break off from the end of the worm in the bowel, and are passed out in the feces. These are sometimes seen around the dog's anus and look like grains of rice. Free-living flea larvae swallow the tapeworm eggs in the environment, and they mature as the flea develops. During normal grooming, the dog swallows the infected flea, and so the life cycle is completed.

Effective tapeworm treatments are available,

but fleas must also be controlled. Unlike roundworms, tapeworms are most usually found in the adult dog. Although it is unpleasant to see egg-packed segments wriggling out of the anus, tapeworm infestation usually has few effects on the normal, healthy adult Boxer.

Heartworm

Dirofilaria immitis is a large worm, up to 11.5 inches (30 cm) in length. They mainly inhabit the pulmonary artery, and the right atrium of the heart, where they cause serious problems. The parasite is transmitted by mosquitoes and is prevalent in many parts of southern Europe and the United States; it is presently absent from Britain. Heartworm is important in Boxers since, as a breed, they can be prone to cardiac problems. Effective prophylactic remedies are available to prevent the onset of heart failure which, at one time, was only too commonly seen in infected dogs.

Hookworms, whipworms, and lungworms

These worms can also cause problems in certain areas. Your local vet will advise if any special remedies or precautions have to be taken.

Endoparasites do not only involve worms. Coccidia, Giardia, and other single-celled organisms can cause problems, especially in kennels. If you are concerned, your vet will be able to advise.

EMERGENCY CARE AND FIRST AID

Emergencies come in all forms – road

Boxers – the canine extroverts – can land themselves in trouble.

accidents, bites, burns, heatstroke, insect stings, allergic reactions, poisoning, and collapse. Boxers – canine extroverts – can often precipitate the unexpected. Be prepared!

First aid is the initial treatment given in an emergency. The purpose is to preserve life, reduce pain and discomfort, and minimize any risk of permanent disability or disfigurement. I hope you will never use the following notes, but it is worthwhile reading them just in case. They are basic principles that can act as your standby when faced with an emergency situation.

All responsible dog owners should learn the principles of first aid.

Priorities:

- Keep calm and try not to panic. If possible get help. Contact your veterinarian if possible, and explain the situation so that you can obtain more specific first aid advice. In the meantime, follow these guidelines.
- If there is possible internal injury, try to keep your dog as still as possible. If your Boxer is unable to stand, try to lay him on the ground and kneel with your arm across his neck so that his head is in contact with the floor. In this way, he is more likely to keep still.
- Shock (see below) is usually part of any emergency. For this, warmth is essential. Try to wrap your dog in whatever is available – blankets, coats; even newspaper is better than nothing.

- Take your dog to the vet as soon as practical. Drive carefully, observe the speed limits and, if possible, take someone with you to keep an eye on the dog while you drive. If he is large, heavy, and cannot walk, try rolling him on a blanket and then two people can carry him between them into the vehicle. Leave the blanket under him so that you can carry him into the veterinarian's office in a similar manner.

Shock

Shock is complex and difficult to define. Primarily due to a lack of fluid in the cells, tissues, or organs of the body, it results in a serious fall in blood pressure.
Causes include:

- Loss of blood due to bleeding
- Heart failure
- Acute allergic reactions

First signs include

- Rapid breathing and heart rate
- Pallor of the mucous membranes of the gums, lips, or under the eyelids
- Feet or ears feel cold to the touch
- Vomiting may occur
- The dog is quiet and unresponsive.

Dealing with shock should include the following measures.

- Try to conserve body heat (see page 121)
- Keep quiet and in a dim light, if possible
- Seek immediate veterinary help
- If necessary, apply the A, B, C of first aid (below).

The A, B, C of First Aid

A   Airway
B   Breathing
C   Cardiac function.

Airway

Injuries to the mouth or throat can happen when playing with a stick, which many Boxers enjoy. If they catch this "end-on," it can result in injury. Collapse or choking can quickly follow.

Breathing can be obstructed. Do your best to clear the mouth and throat in order to allow the passage of as much air (oxygen) to the lungs as possible. To do this, however, you must take care.

DO NOT PUT YOUR HAND IN YOUR BOXER'S MOUTH

Remember, he will be just as terrified as you are and, if he is fighting for his breath, he may well bite in panic. Use any blunt object, e.g., a piece of wood, the handle of a small gardening tool etc., to try and open the mouth. Then, with a piece of cloth wrapped around the piece of stick or similar object, you can often clear any obstruction from the mouth.

Breathing

If your dog has collapsed and is not breathing, lay him on his side with both forelegs pulled forward. With both hands, try gently pushing the chest just behind the elbow. At the same time, try to detect a heartbeat (pulse) at approximately the same position. If no heartbeat can be detected, move swiftly on to cardiac massage (see below).

Cardiac function

In a normal Boxer, the cardiac pulse (heartbeat) can often be seen between the ribs on the left side, just behind the elbow. Feeling in that area will detect the heartbeat, even if it is not visible. If you cannot detect a heartbeat, try gently squeezing the ribs in this area, 15 to 20 times a minute, stopping every half minute or so, to check for a pulse. If there is no sign, continue the squeezing. This is external cardiac massage. Try to pull the tongue forward, and if it is cyanosed (blue), place a handkerchief over the mouth and nose, and try blowing down his throat and nose while continuing chest massage.

COMMON PROBLEMS

Anaphylaxis

(Hives, nettle rash, or acute allergic reaction.) Boxers are allergy prone; nettle rash (hives) type swellings can develop very quickly. Insect stings (bees, wasps, hornets), plant stings, or dietary allergies can all be responsible. It is very frightening if your pet's face suddenly swells to twice its normal size before your eyes, but usually the swellings disappear as quickly as they come. The danger is if breathing is compromised, in part due to the flat Boxer face. Sometimes the swellings are extremely pruritic (itchy), and the rubbing and scratching make the condition worse.

Bathe with cold water. Apply antihistamine cream if available, and go to your vet as soon as possible. An antihistamine injection usually results in a rapid response.

Bleeding

The lively Boxer may cut his feet on broken glass in parks and recreation grounds. If bleeding is severe, improvise a bandage from any available clean material. A polythene bag applied between the layers of bandage will keep the blood contained. The aim is to prevent blood loss. Get your dog to the vet as soon as possible. If you have bandaged the limb very tightly, make sure it is not left on for more than 15 or 20 minutes without rebandaging.

If hemorrhage is from an area where bandaging is impractical, for example a bite wound to the throat or lips, endeavor to control the bleeding by applying finger or hand pressure, preferably with a piece of clean dressing material, soaked in cold water, held between your hand and the wound.

Burns and scalds

Cool the burned area with cold water as quickly as possible. If the affected area is extensive, use wet towels. If the injury is due to a caustic substance, wash away as much of this as you can with plenty of cold water. If the burn is in the mouth, press cloths, soaked in clean, cold water, between the jaws.

Eye injuries

Foreign bodies, usually grass awns and scratches either from cats' claws or bushes, are not

Keep a close check on your Boxer's eyes as problems can occur if foreign bodies, such as grass awns, enter the eye.

uncommon problems affecting Boxers' eyes. Usually the dog returns with the eye tightly closed, resenting handling. If you cannot easily see the cause of the problem, cover the eye with a pad soaked in cold water or, better still, in saline solution (e.g., contact lens solution), and seek veterinary help without delay.

Fits and seizures

Convulsions, fits, or seizures can and do occur in the Boxer. They may happen following head injury or they may occur spontaneously as a form of epilepsy. Although it is very frightening for the onlooker, remember that your dog does not know what is happening. The less you handle him, the less stimulation he has and the greater the chance the problem will rapidly resolve. If possible, place him in a dark, confined area where he cannot damage himself.

Most seizures only last a few seconds or minutes. It is better to wait until there has been some recovery before going to the vet. If the seizure continues for more than three or four minutes, contact your vet immediately and seek instructions.

Heatstroke

Heatstroke is the all too frequent result of dogs being left in cars with too little ventilation in sultry weather. Remember, the car does not need to be in direct sunlight to kill your dog. Body temperature rises rapidly and this soon results in irreversible damage. Signs start with panting and obvious distress. Unconsciousness and coma quickly follow.

A car can heat up rapidly, even when it is not left in direct sunlight.

Try to reduce body temperature as quickly as possible. Bathe your Boxer in copious amounts of cold water. If ice is available, place it on the head, under the tail, and between the legs. Wrap the still wet animal in damp towels and take him to the vet without delay.

BREED-SPECIFIC PROBLEMS

This immensely popular, adaptable, working dog does have some breed-associated problems. Some, of course, are shared with all the flat-faced (brachycephalic) dogs, but other conditions definitely seem to be breed-specific.

Allergies

Boxers are allergy prone. Following some injections, for example, they can occasionally develop hives or nettle rash, with weals and rashes developing very rapidly. These usually

Boxers have a tendency to suffer allergic reactions.

disappear just as quickly following an antihistamine injection from your vet. Wasps, bees, and other stinging insects can elicit equally dramatic reactions, and these can result in an emergency if swelling makes breathing difficult.

More insidious and difficult to treat is the Boxer with atopic disease, often an inherited predisposition to react to certain environmental allergens such as pollen. The presenting sign is usually intense itching. If due to pollens, this can be seasonal. Sometimes, only the ears are affected. Some Boxers have bowel upsets and chronic diarrhea due to food allergies and will require lifelong diet control following careful diagnosis. In short, if your Boxer has any unexplained acute swelling, itching, or bowel problems, see your vet with a view to investigation.

Cancer

There are certain tumors which occur more frequently in the Boxer than in other breeds. Mast cell tumors (MCT) can occur throughout the body, but in the Boxer they are frequently associated with skin cancers. They often appear quite suddenly, and they are often mistaken for a sting. They release histamines and can cause acute inflammation and intense itching. The appearance of any sudden lumps or bumps in your Boxer indicates a trip to the vet, if only to put your mind at rest.

Other tumors

Older Boxers sometimes develop signs similar to stroke in people, often due to space-occupying tumors in the brain. Usually very slow growing; palliative treatment is often effective.

Epuli

These are tumors growing from the gums. A single epulus can result in bleeding, ulceration, and loosening of a tooth to an extent requiring surgery. Regular dental checks are always worthwhile with Boxers.

Eye problems

There are several eye problems of concern, but these are not currently subject to eradication programs. They appear more generally associated with the brachycephalic (short-faced) anatomy than an inherent breed problem.

Indolent ulcer

Probably the most important and most painful

Ask your vet to give your puppy a routine heart check.

condition is corneal ulceration – indolent ulcer. This occurs mainly in middle-aged and older Boxers. The ulcer is often resistant to the usual forms of medical treatment. There are very effective surgical techniques carried out by veterinary ophthalmologists.

Distichiasis

This is congenital – present from birth. The dog has a double row of eyelashes which may rub on the eyeball and thus initiate the corneal ulcer. This is a problem which needs attention earlier rather than later, using a veterinarian experienced in eye problems.

Other eye conditions that can occur are entropion (inturning) or ectropion (sagging) eyelids. Rubbing due to irritation can result in ulceration. Boxers can also have fatty material (usually cholesterol) in the cornea. Other

Keep a close check on your Boxer, so you can spot any signs of ill health at an early stage.

The athletic Boxer rarely suffers skeletal problems.

conditions can cause clouding of the whole cornea. If you are at all worried about your Boxer's eyes, consult your vet without delay.

Heart problems

Unfortunately, Boxers have more than their fair share of congenital heart conditions. Aortic stenosis, the most common, affects the left side of the heart. Pulmonic stenosis, which is less common, affects mainly the pulmonary artery and then the right side of the heart.

Both can lead to cardiac enlargement, and, if very severe, may result in unexpected heart failure.

Dilated cardiomyopathy (DCM) can occur on its own, or as a sequel to stenosis. In the Boxer, it usually results in enlargement of the left ventricle. Frequently, the abnormality is only detected on routine cardiac examination.

These conditions sound very frightening, but modern drugs can work miracles, stabilizing if not curing many of these conditions. However, it is prudent, when first presenting your puppy to the vet, to ensure that a routine heart check is carried out.

Skeletal problems

Generally, the athletic, muscular Boxer does not suffer from skeletal problems. According to the Orthopaedic Foundation for Animals Scheme, the Boxer is placed in 73rd position in their league table of breeds affected by hip dysplasia. The British Veterinary Association/Kennel Club Scheme gives a breed average hip score of 16.

There are always exceptions, though. If your Boxer shows any signs of stiffness, lameness, or skeletal or joint pain, seek immediate veterinary advice.

With good care, your Boxer should live a long, happy, and healthy life.

Other breed-prone conditions

Hypothyroidism, resulting in a reduction in circulating thyroid hormones, results in decreased energy levels, obesity and poor coat growth.

Seasonal flank alopecia occurs in dogs of either sex. The hairlessness affecting both flanks frequently starts in autumn and usually resolves spontaneously in spring and summer. Ulcerative colitis affects young Boxers and can result in chronic diarrhea. It appears to be an immune mediated disease.

If you have any concerns regarding problems with your Boxer, call your vet sooner rather than later.

FINAL NOTE

A chapter on health care always leaves the impression that the breed in question is prone to all sorts of problems. But, fortunately, with the Boxer this is very far from the case. Developed by canine experts to be a super-breed, the Boxer has the advantages of an athletic physique and a hardy constitution. With good care, you can be confident that your Boxer will give you many years of trouble-free companionship.